ANCIENT WORLD
COMMANDERS

ANCIENT WORLD COMMANDERS

FROM THE TROJAN WAR TO THE FALL OF ROME

ANGUS KONSTAM

COMPENDIUM

This 2008 edition published by

COMPENDIUM

© 2008 by Compendium
Publishing Ltd. 43 Frith Street,
London W1D 4SA, United Kingdom

Project Manager: Ray Bonds
Designer: Cara Rogers
Color Reproduction:
Anorax Imaging Ltd

ISBN: 978-1-906347-29-1

Printed and bound in China

Contents

Additional illustrations

Page 1: A marble bust of the Roman Emperor Septimus Severus (reigned 146-211 AD).

Previous pages: The Death of Julius Caesar, a painting by Vincenzo Carnuccini, c.1793.

Left: The Greek hero Ulysses, tied to the mast of his ship during his epic voyage, shown in a 3rd century AD Roman fresco from Dougga, Tunisia.

Introduction

The "Ancient World" is a modern catch-all phrase, a form of historical shorthand that covers roughly two-and-a-half thousand years of human activity. The historical injustice of this is self-evident—imagine just how much has happened in the past five hundred years, since the Renaissance. It seems almost derisory to place a period five times as extensive into a single historical package. However, this approach is not without its advantages. This book looks at military leaders—some have remained household names despite the passage of the millennia, while others have rightly or wrongly been forgotten in the passage of time. By grouping together these commanders we can learn something of the development of the military art, and the way these military thinkers viewed the world in which they lived and fought.

The period encompassed in this book runs from the dawn of recorded history—around the start of the second millennium BC—to the century following the collapse of the Roman World in the early 5th century AD. Some historians have happily extended the period further, either drawing on the scanty evidence of military organizations in the Middle East before the creation of written records, or following the development of military activity in Europe and elsewhere beyond the collapse of the Roman Empire. However, the "ancient" world is as determined as much by

Left: King Darius III of Persia in his chariot, fleeing from the Battle of Issus. In the background can be seen the pikes of Alexander the Great's victorious Macedonian infantry. A detail from a Roman mosaic dating from the 2nd-1st centuries BC, House of Faun, Pompeii.

society, trade, civilization, and culture as it is by warfare. The collapse of the certainties of the Roman way of life marked a major change in the way armies were organized, and how they fought. Therefore it makes a sensible place to bring our catch-all period to an end.

Of course, this is much more than a simple list of who did what, and where they fought. Each of these commanders fought according to the constraints of the time, using the army created by contemporary society. This meant that the armies used by the Ancient Egyptians had a completely different composition to those that fought under Alexander the Great, or Caesar, or Attila "the Hun". The way these military leaders used their armies in battle reveals a lot about their own martial abilities, and a little more about the effectiveness of their military machine. By comparing the armies and commanders of different historical phases within our catch-all "Ancient" period we can also trace the evolution of warfare and military thought during the first two-and-a-half thousand years of recorded history.

Whether or not you accept the premise that mankind is essentially aggressive, we can assume that some form of warfare took place before the beginning of recorded human activity. Stone Age tribesmen almost certainly clashed with other groups, using whatever weapons they had to hand. Archaeological evidence supports this since traces of Neolithic fortifications have been found in Jericho on the West Bank of the River Jordan, dated to around 6,000 BC, some four thousand years before Egyptian written records provide us with the first historical account of a

Left: A reconstruction of an Egyptian wall painting depicts the two-wheeled chariots that formed the core of a New Kingdom period army.

Right: The bronze armor of a Mycenaean Greek warrior, from Dendra in Greece, and dating from the 12th century BC—the time of the Trojan War.

military engagement. Weapons have been found in the Middle East dating from the middle of the 4th millennium BC, while similar finds in the Indus Valley of India and the Yellow River in China also predate the first historical records.

The first descriptions of military conflict provide us with general accounts of wars, the migration of peoples, and the conquest of states, but by the start of the "Middle Bronze Age" in the Middle East—around 1,500 BC, these records begin to flesh out the details, revealing information about the commanders and their armies, and how they were used in battle. The first recorded battle in history was Megiddo, fought in 1,469 BC between the Egyptians and the Palestinians, when the Pharaoh Thutmosis III routed his opponents. Warfare during this Egyptian "New Kingdom" period involved the use of both shock weapons, such as spears and swords, and missile weapons in the form of bows and slings. Soldiers wore protective armor, while Egyptian written records show that troops were formed into recognizable formations. Mobility was provided by the horse-drawn chariot, which formed the main striking force of most armies until the 7th century BC. Cavalry—a military development pioneered by the Assyrians—began to appear around 1,000 BC.

Of course, the Middle East wasn't the only area where military developments were taking place. There were many parallels. The Early Chinese, for instance, relied on chariots, bows, and spears to win their battles, while Chinese metallurgical technology is believed to have been more advanced than in the Middle East, such that the development of armor advanced further and faster in the Far East than elsewhere. By the 6th century BC the Chinese had developed a highly organized military system, whose steps from platoons and companies up to divisions and corps would easily be recognized today. Similar devel-

Below: Greek hoplites—closely formed armored infantry equipped with spear and shield, from a detail of a 6th century BC Greek vase.

opments were taking place in India, although horses were rare, so that massed formations of chariots were unknown.

These early centuries were essentially a formative period, but by around 600 BC a style of weaponry had evolved that—with only minor changes—would remain in vogue throughout the "Ancient" period. However, the employment of these weapons on the battlefield improved significantly as new theories on tactics and doctrine were

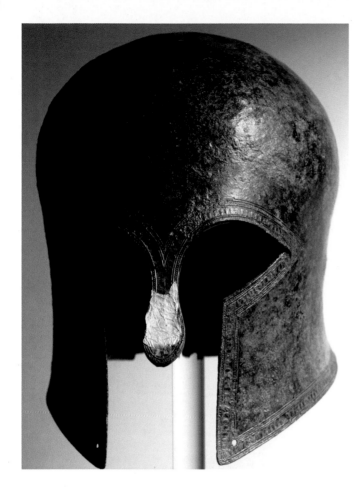

demanded an improvement in the logistical and administrative organization of these military forces. In Ancient Greece the first military theorists—men such as Herodotus and Thucydides—began to address these problems, as too did the famous Chinese strategist Sun Tzu, whose *The Art of War* remains a classic military text.

By the start of the 5th century BC the development of military tactics and organization was well advanced. In effect it provided a tool for kings and generals to conduct ever-more ambitious military campaigns, where strategic rather than limited tactical or operational goals could be set, and where warfare could be conducted on a hitherto

Above: The bronze helmet of a Greek hoplite, in the Corinthian style, dating from the 6th century BC, discovered in the necropolis of Haghia Paraskevi in northern Greece.
Right: A heavily decorated and gilded bronze cuirass of Phoenician origin, discovered in Ksour-es-Saf, Tunisia. It was probably once worn by a Carthaginian soldier.

developed. Just as important, the way armies were managed went through a transformation between 600–400 BC, as national economies developed to the extent that they could support large armies and fleets, which in turn unimaginably large scale. The period from around 400–200 BC was dominated by some of the greatest military figures in history—leaders of the stature of Alexander the Great, Hannibal, and Scipio Africanus. These men engaged in conflicts in which military might was supported by warfare using diplomatic and economic stratagems, and where grand strategies were made possible because these leaders could rely on the military forces at their disposal to achieve what was asked of them.

This was also a time of military innovation. Alexander's father, Philip II, had introduced light infantrymen into his army, while his Greek rivals developed the siege machines that would become a vital part of military campaigning in the Ancient world. Alexander encountered military elephants in India, while Hannibal employed African elephants in the army with which he crossed the Alps. It was Alexander who was credited with the development of shock cavalry—a battle-winning force that his Persian opponents found impossible to beat. Similarly, his father's infantry developed a new set of tactics that centered on the use of the pike. Under Alexander these Macedonian pikemen were turned into a highly efficient military instrument.

When Alexander entered India he encountered a military system that had developed along slightly different lines, based on the military and governmental theories enshrined in the *Arthasastra*. In contrast with the peoples of the Mediterranean, the Indian Mauryan Emperors relied on standing armies, raised and paid for by means of a complex, semi-feudal system. Similarly, the Chinese developed their own military structure during this period, and their soldiers are preserved for posterity in the "terracotta armies" that provide us with a fascinating visual image of how these soldiers looked, and how they were armed. What they fail to reveal is the highly sophisticated way these armies were organized and run. The Chinese rulers of this period managed to develop a method of military

organization and administration that would be unmatched in the West until the arrival of the Romans.

The wars fought between Rome and Carthage revealed the problems inherent in the Roman military system. The army itself was a force of Roman citizens, whose exclusivity limited its ability to replace battlefield losses. These Roman armies were commanded by men who were statesmen first and military commanders second, and who—despite the emergence of leaders of the caliber of Scipio Africanus—were forced to concentrates as much on the political situation back in Rome as they did on the activities of their enemies. However, these leaders and armies were supported by a formidable military bureaucracy, and the Romans themselves possessed a will to win that often overcame many of the obstacles placed in the path of military success.

It was the veteran general Gaius Marius who transformed this Roman army into a force capable of conquering the known world. He opened its ranks to all Roman citizens, regardless of social standing, and in the process he created a professional standing army. Although its ranks were now drawn from the lower orders of society, these men were trained to become experts in their deadly craft. At the same time, Marius restructured the army organization, creating efficient tactical units, and provided these troops with the best weapons available. The result was the Roman legionary, a troop type who would dominate Ancient history for the best part of five centuries.

The only flaw in Marius' creation was that now soldiers owed their loyalty as much to the leader who raised

Right: Roman soldiers in a detail from the Arch of Constantine in Rome, which was erected in 315 AD to commemorate the Emperor Constantine's victory over his Imperial rival Maxentius three years earlier. However, it incorporated earlier Roman bas-relief sculptures, including this 2nd century AD panel depicting an incident in the Dacian Wars, a carving that may well have been taken from Trajan's Column.

Left: Roman legionaries operating a ballista (bolt-thrower) during the Siege of Alesia (52 BC), where Julius Caesar crushed the revolt led by the Gallic chieftain Vercingetorix. Caesar's victory was due in part to the technological superiority of the Roman army over their Gallic foes.

the legion in which they served as to the Roman state. Consequently, the decades that followed saw the destruction of the Roman Republic, crushed under the boots of the legionaries commanded by the likes of Marius, Sulla, Pompey, Caesar, and even the future Emperor Augustus. Even after the transition from Republic into Empire the Roman military machine remained a constant threat to the stability of the very society it was paid to protect. The history of the Roman Empire from the 1st century until the early 5th century AD is littered with accounts of Roman armies marching on the capital, and emperors created or replaced at the whim of the army.

Given this political record it is surprising that the Roman army remained such a formidable military machine for so long. It collapsed only under the weight of the Barbarian Invasions of the late 4th and early 5th centuries AD, when the Roman bureaucratic structure failed to support the organization and administration of the army, and when the professionalism of the force had been diluted by the recruitment of non-Roman troops. While the Sack of Rome by the Visigoths didn't mark the end of the Roman World, it presaged the collapse of the Western Roman Empire, and ushered in the era that is popularly known as the "Dark Ages." While military innovations continued in the Eastern Mediterranean, in India and in China, the Ancient World as most people now define it was no more.

Probably the single most lasting legacy of all these centuries of warfare is the example provided by the men who commanded these ancient armies, whose achievements still have a resonance today. These leaders came from variety of backgrounds, either acquiring their positions as army commanders through royal succession, through elec-

tion by their peers, or simply by removing any political rivals who stood in their way.

A quick look at some of the greatest leaders of this period—as named above—reveals that despite their path to command, all of them shared certain abilities when they assumed the role of army commander, such as being able to inspire others to make the best use of the military units at their disposal. These aptitudes are just as important to military or business leaders today as they were then.

This survey of ancient military commanders is by no means exhaustive, but it includes virtually everyone whose presence on an ancient battlefield made a difference to the outcome of the battle, or whose triumphs or defeats have reverberated through history. All of them—whether successful and famous, or unsuccessful and obscure—play a part in building up the tapestry of ancient military achievement. This book can be used simply to trace the career of an individual figure from ancient military history, or the list can be viewed as a tool that can place these leaders in a wider context, tracing the early development of history through the activities of the commanders who first defined the military art.

Achilles
Trojan War (mythological)
Greek Hero

Aeneas
Trojan War (mythological)
Trojan Hero

Born of an immortal mother, Achilles was the great hero of the *Iliad*. He abandoned the Greeks during the Trojan War, but eventually rejoined them on the brink of defeat and killed Hector, the Trojan hero. Achilles was then, in some accounts, killed by an arrow to the heel, fired by Paris, Hector's brother.

Above: Achilles, from the marble sculpture Ludovisi Ares, a Roman copy of a Greek original, which was subsequently restored by Bernini.

The son of King Priam, mentioned in Homer's *Iliad* and Virgil's *Aeneid*, Aeneas escaped the sacking of Troy and fled to Carthage where he had an affair with Queen Dido. He eventually arrived in Italy with his followers and became progenitor of Rome. Aeneas founded the city of Lavinium and was granted immortality by Jupiter.

Above: The Goddess Venus appearing before Aeneas, in a fresco by Giambattista Tiepolo.

Agamemnon
Trojan War (mythalogical)
Greek General and King

Possibly a mythical rather than historical figure, Agamemnon was commander of the Greek army during the Trojan Wars. He quarreled with Achilles, who damaged Greek chances by withdrawing from battle. Agamemnon fought heroically but was wounded in battle. On his return home he was murdered by his wife Clytemnestra, who had taken a lover.

Above: Agamemnon preparing to leave for Troy (depicted on Greek vase).

Above: A golden mask, said to have belonged to Agamemnon, recovered from a tomb in Mycenae in Greece.

Gnaeus Julius Agricola
(40-93 AD)
Imperial Roman General

Agricola was born into a noble roman family in the province of Gallia Narbonensis (now the South of France), his father being a Senator who had fallen foul of the Emperor Caligula. Around 56 AD he entered military service as a tribune, and from 58-62 he served on the staff of Gaius Suetonius Paulinus, the conqueror and first governor of Roman Britain. Agricola saw active service during the suppression of Boudica's revolt in 61 AD, and the following year he was

stationed in Rome, where after an astute marriage he was made a Quaestor, and sent to Asia Minor to assist the provincial governor. During 68 AD—"The Year of the Four Emperors"—Agricola supported the victorious Imperial candidate Vespasian, and was rewarded with command of the XX Legion, which was stationed in Britain.

Between 70 and 74 AD he conducted a highly successful campaign against the Brigantes in what is now Northern England, and after being briefly recalled to Rome Agricola returned to Britain in 78 AD, this time as governor. He immediately launched an offensive against the Ordovices in Wales, and subdued the region after capturing the British island stronghold of Mona (now Anglesey). He also developed a reputation as a sound administrator and builder. Then in 80 AD he launched his invasion of Caledonia (now Scotland), driving northwards past the line of the Rivers Forth and Clyde into the Highlands. He finally managed to bring the Caledonii and their leader Calgacus to bay somewhere near Bennachie, to the west of the modern city of Aberdeen. In the Battle of Mons Graupius (84 AD) that followed he successfully crushed Caledonian resistance and forced his enemies to scatter into the Highlands.

Having subdued but not fully conquered Scotland, Agricola established outposts to guard his northern borders, then returned south. He had proved a highly capable commander—and therefore a possible threat. In 85 AD he was recalled to Rome by the Emperor Domitian, who allowed his general to hold a triumphal parade, but not to hold any further military command. Agricola died on his family estates eight years later.

Left: A 17th century depiction of Julius Agricola, with the Roman fleet supporting his advance through Britain.

Agrippa, Marcus Vipsanius
(63-12 BC)
Republican Roman General

Supported Octavian after Caesars death, fought at Philippi in 42BC, became governor of Gaul where he suppressed a rebellion in 38BC. Agrippa fought the German tribes across the Rhine, destroyed the fleet of Sextus in 36BC and delivered victory to Octavian in 31BC at the Battle of Actium. He died campaigning on the Danube at the age of 51.

Above: Roman aqueduct, the Pont du Gard in Nimes, France, one of several built under the supervision of Marcus Agrippa.
Left: Roman coin showing (right) Marcus Agrippa, alongside friend and mentor Octavian, the future Emperor Augustus.

Alaric
(c.370–410 AD),
King of the Visigoths

The first barbarian leader to sack Rome, Alaric was reputedly born on Peuce, an island in the Danube Estuary, now part of Romania. The Germanic people known as the Goths were divided into two groups—Alaric's people, the Visigoths (Western Goths), and the Ostrogoths. Both originated in Eastern Europe, but by

the time of Alaric's birth the Visigoths had settled in what is now Romania and Bulgaria, migrating south to avoid the Huns. As a young man Alaric served as a *foederati*, a barbarian soldier in service of the Roman Empire. From 382 AD the Ostrogoths had been allowed to settle within the frontiers of the Eastern Roman Empire, so played an active part in its defense.

In 394 AD Alaric served under the Emperor Theodosius I, and the Visigoth almost certainly fought at the Battle of the Frigidus (394 AD), which

Above: Alaric, King of the Visigoths, in a 19th century depiction of the sack of Rome.
Right: A more stately 19th century rendering of Alaric's first entry into Rome, at the invitation of its citizens.

pitched two Roman armies against each other, but which resulted in a victory that allowed Theodosius to temporarily reunite the divided Roman world. The emperor died the following year and the territory was divided between his two sons, Arcadius, who ruled the east, and the young Honorius, who became the

into Greece. The bulk of the Eastern Roman army was busy fighting the Huns in Asia Minor and Syria, so Stilicho marched east to help. However, Arcadius was dominated by his leading minister, Rufinus, who may well have been in league with the Visigoths, so the eastern emperor ordered Stilicho to halt his advance in Illyria (now Croatia). Alaric was therefore given a free hand to ravage Greece, enslaving the citizens of all the major cities apart from Athens, which was spared following its surrender in 396 AD.

This was too much for Stilicho, who ignored Arcadius and invaded Greece in 397 AD. Alaric managed to avoid being trapped by Stilicho and escaped to the north, continuing his rampage in Illyria. Arcadius tried to restore order by making Alaric a provincial governor, but Alaric continued marching west, and in 401 AD he entered Italy. His ravaging of northern Italy was stopped by Stilicho, who caught up with the Visigoths at Pollentia (now Pollenza) in 402 AD. The Romans won a costly victory, and Alaric withdrew to the east, his progress encouraged by a second defeat near Verona the following year. Alaric bided his time in Illyria, playing the two emperors against each other. Then in 408 AD the Emperor Honorius had Stilicho killed, along with most of his *foederati*. Barbarians in the pay of the western empire flocked into Alaric's camp, giving him the manpower he needed to return to Italy.

This second Visigothic invasion was virtually unopposed, and in September 408 AD Alaric laid siege to Rome. The emperor was safely ensconced in Ravenna, and the Romans were left to their own devices. However, Alaric had no wish to capture the city, only to exact favorable terms for his people. The Romans paid the Visigothic leader an immense ransom, and the siege was duly lifted. The Visigoths moved north again, as Alaric continued to try to negotiate with the emperor in an attempt to secure a safe homeland for his people. When these talks broke down Alaric reluctantly marched south again, and in 409 AD the Visigoths laid siege to Rome a second time. The Romans elected a rival emperor, who negotiated a truce. However, when he proved ineffective, Alaric deposed him, marched north again, and reopened negotiations with Honorius.

Once again the emperor broke his word, so in August

Above: Alaric depicted as the noble barbarian, protecting Rome's citizens from the worst ravages of his Goths.

western emperor. As Honorius was too young to rule his part of the empire directly, his father had requested that the veteran General Stilicho act as his regent. Alaric hoped this change of power would benefit his people, but when the Visigoths were ignored by both young emperors he decided to take matters into his own hands.

He attacked the Eastern Roman Empire first, his Visigoths advancing to the very walls of the imperial capital of Byzantium (Constantinople, now Istanbul). However, the Visigoths lacked the siege equipment needed to capture the city, so they moved west through Thessaly and

ALARICVS

Above: Alaric, king of the Visigoths.
Right: The sack of Rome by the Visigoths, 410 AD.

410 AD Alaric marched on Rome a third time. His Visigoths broke through the northern walls near the Porta Salaria, and the city fell. Rome had at last been conquered. His men looted the city, but Alaric reputedly kept the destruction to a minimum. The Visigoths then marched south into Calbria, which Alaric hoped to use as a springboard for an invasion of Africa, another attempt to secure a prosperous Visigoth homeland. However, Alaric died of fever in late 410 AD, before any invasion could be attempted. Ironically, he was succeeded by his brother-in-law Ataulf, who in 413 AD married the sister of the Emperor Honorius. Five years later the emperor finally granted the Visigoths the homeland they craved, in southern Gaul and Spain, which remained in Visigothic hands until the 8th century AD.

Alcibiades

(450–40 BC)
Athenian General and Statesman

Alcibiades was born into an aristocratic family in Athens in 450 BC. In his early military career he fought in the Battle of Potidaea (432 BC) where Socrates saved his life, a favor that he returned while fighting in Delium in 424 BC. Alcibiades came to prominence in 422 BC when he became a general following successful political maneuverings against Sparta. However, Alcibiades was embroiled in a religious scandal involving the mutilation of a statue of Hermes and was tried and sentenced to death.

Alcibiades escaped his sentence and was granted sanctuary by the Spartans who he repaid with military advice that helped the Spartans win several victories, including the defeat of the Athenians in Sicily. But Alcibiades soon fell out of favor when his affair with the wife of the Spartan king was uncovered. It was not until 411 BC that Alcibiades was allowed to return from exile where he took part in several successful sea battles, but his career ended in defeat when the Spartan general Lysander destroyed the Athenian fleet at Notium (406 BC). Alcibiades was removed from command and was murdered the following year. Although Alcibiades was certainly an ambitious and successful general, many regarded him as unscrupulous and a traitor whose confidence exceeded his skills.

Above: Alcibiades, as depicted in a Grecian marble bust in the Museo Capitolino in Rome.

Alexander "the Great"
(336-323 BC)
King of Macedon

Above: Battle between the Greeks and Persians; relief from the Alexander Sarcophagus from Sidon.

Alexander, the son of King Philip II of Macedon, was born in the Macedonian capital of Pella, in what is now northern Greece, although Greek historians later claimed the young prince was sired by the god Zeus rather than by the king. He was raised in the court, and educated by the best tutors available, including Aristotle, who cultivated Alexander's interest in the arts and sciences. It is claimed that when the boy was aged ten a horse trader brought a wild black stallion to Pella, which nobody was able to tame apart from Alexander himself. Alexander named the horse Bucephalis, and the two became inseparable companions.

Above: The Macedonian army of Alexander the Great, shown crossing the rivers Euphrates and Tigris during his conquest of Mesopotamia, from a 15th century illustration.

Alexander was equally loyal to his childhood friends, particularly Hephaestion, and by the time he had become a teenager the prince had welded these youngsters into a loyal bodyguard—"The Companions."
In 338 BC Alexander fought alongside his father at the Battle of Chaeronea, an engagement that secured Macedonian domination over the Greek city states. King Philip then planned to campaign against the Persians, but in 336 BC he was assassinated, a deed that may well have been ordered by the Persian King. If so, then King Darius III underestimated Philip's son. The twenty-year-old Alexander was crowned King of Macedonia, and moved swiftly to quell unrest in Greece. He then moved north into Thrace, securing the northern boundaries of Macedonia. All was now ready for his campaign against Persia.

In 334 BC Alexander then led his army of 42,000 men across the Hellespont into Asia, and at the Battle of Granicus defeated the Persian army sent to stop him. After capturing the regional capital of Sardis he marched south, down the Ionian coast of Asia Minor to the city of Halicarnassus, which he besieged and captured. Next he led his troops eastwards along the coast, capturing other ports, and so denying them to the Persians. Then he turned north into the Phrygian plain, and as winter arrived his army had reached the city of Gordium. It was said that whoever could unravel the rope puzzle known as the

"Gordian knot" would become the King of Asia. Alexander solved the problem by slicing it in two with his sword.

Early the following year Alexander led his Macedonians through the mountainous Cilician Gates to the coastal plain, where he defeated King Darius and his main army at the Battle of Issus. The Persian king fled, leaving his family and treasury behind him. The Macedonian king followed up his victory by marching down the Mediterranean coast, besieging and capturing Tyre, then working his way south to Gaza. There he was welcomed as the liberator of Egypt, and a god—the son of Zeus-Ammon. He founded the city of Alexandria, then led his army eastwards again into Assyria (now northern Iraq). It was there that he defeated a third Persian army at the Battle of Gaugamela (331 BC), and once again Darius fled the field. Alexander pursued him as far as Arabela, then marched south to capture Babylon and then east again to secure the regional capital of Susa and the Persian royal capital of Persepolis. He was now able to legitimately sit on Darius' throne.

The Persian king was murdered by Bessus, a Bactrian ruler who proclaimed himself King Artaxerxes V of Persia. Alexander set out to crush his new rival, and in a campaign that

Below: The Triumph of Alexander the Great— entry into Babylon, painted by Charles Le Brun, 1665.
Following pages: The Battle of Issus, Alexander's great victory over the Persians, as depicted in a 16th century painting.

Above: The Continence of Alexander the Great, from a painting by Giambattista Tiepolo.

marching down the Indus to the sea, and then marching westward through the desert to Persia. The march was grueling, and thousands of his men perished before they reached the haven of the Persian capital. Alexander planned to lead his army on further campaigns, but the young god proved mortal after all, and died in Persepolis in June 323 BC, aged just thirty-three. He left behind a sprawling empire, which was soon divided up by his successors. However, his achievements were such that today Alexander "the Great" is regarded as the greatest ancient commander of them all.

Below: The young Alexander in the Macedonian court, alongside his father King Philip and his mother Olympias (from a 14th century Byzantine illustration).

lasted for three years he went on to conquer Media, Parthia, Bactria, and Sogdiana. By 328 BC Artaxerxes was dead, and Alexander's army found itself in what is now Afghanistan. Alexander now ruled most of the known world, but he decided to continue into India, which he regarded as a land of plenty. By this time many of his Greek and Macedonian troops simply wanted to go home, and resented the way their king embraced Persian dress and customs. Alexander thwarted two plots against him, and killed those responsible.

He cemented his hold over Central Asia by marrying the Bactrian princess Roxana, and so in 326 BC he was able to march south through the Afghan mountains to India. He eventually emerged in the plains of what is now Pakistan, and it was there that he defeated an Indian army led by the local ruler, Porus, at the Battle of Hydaspes. He now controlled the headwaters of the Indus River, and he wanted to press into the sub-continent. However, his troops refused to follow him, and Alexander had no option but to turn back. He decided to return to Persepolis by

Ambiorix
(c.54 BC)
Gallic Chief of the Eburones

Amenhotep III
(1391-1353 BC)
Egyptian Pharaoh

Amboiorix joined forces with Catuvolcus and led the Eburones tribe against the Romans of Julius Caesar, managing to destroy an entire legion and five cohorts. Caesar's response involved 50,000 Roman troops and a campaign lasting several years. The tribes were exterminated but Amboiorix and his force managed to escape across the Rhine.

Above: Ambiorix, chief of the Eburones, in a bronze statue in Tongeren, Belgium.

Amenhotep reigned during a period of unprecedented affluence, artistic grandeur, and political power. He was responsible for extensive building, including the Luxor Temple, and his mortuary temple on the Nile was the largest religious complex in Thebes. Amenhotep died in his 'forties with Egypt at the height of its power.

Above: The Pharaoh Amenhotep III, shown wearing the crown of Upper Egypt, in a fragment of a larger granite statue found at his tomb in Qurna.

Antigonus I (Monophthalmus)
(c.382-301 BC)
Macedonian General and King

Antigonus fought in the successor wars after the death of Alexander the Great, He tried to reunite Alexander's empire, but was eventually defeated by the combined forces of Seleucus and Lysimachus at Ipsus in 301 BC, Antigonus was killed by a javelin at the age of eighty-one, in the first battle he ever lost.

Above: Antigones I, as depicted on a Greek coin, with the God Zeus on the reverse.

Antiochus III "the Great"
(241-197 BC, reigned 223-187 BC)
King of Seleucia

The teenage Antiochus succeeded his brother Seleucus, who was assassinated in 223 BC, and thereby inherited a kingdom in turmoil. Asia Minor had seceded, as had Bactria and Parthia, while Persia and Judea were in revolt. In 221 BC he campaigned in Media and Persia, using force to end the revolt there. Antiochus then subjugated Judea, and by 218 BC his armies faced those of Ptolemy IV of Egypt. The two sides clashed the following year, and in 217

Right: Antiochus III "the Great," in a marble bust in the Louvre.

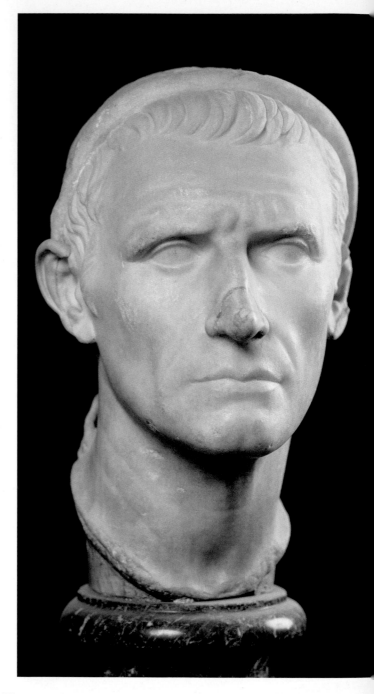

BC Antiochus was defeated at the Battle of Raphia, forcing him to withdraw back into Syria. In 214 BC the Seleucid king crushed the rebellion in Asia Minor by capturing the rebel stronghold of Sardis. With Asia Minor secure he then marched east, and in 212 BC he forced the Armenians to become a client state. Three years later the Parthians did the same. Next Antiochus invaded Bactria, whose king was forced to negotiate a peace treaty when Antiochus besieged his capital. Before returning west the Seleucid king campaigned in Afghanistan, and protected his eastern borders by cementing an alliance with the Indian king Sophagasenus.

Antiochus still had unfinished business with the Egyptians, and so in 199 BC he invaded the Ptolemaic provinces of Phoenecia and Judaea, and his subsequent victory at the Battle of Panium (198 BC) restored these lost provinces to the Seleucid Empire. The following year he led his army into Asia Minor to secure the coastal cities that had offered their allegiance to the Egyptians, and when Smyrna asked the Romans for help Antiochus found himself at war with a far more formidable opponent. Urged on by the exiled Carthaginian Hannibal, Antiochus invaded Greece in 192 BC, but his defeat at the hands of a Roman army at Thermopylae (191 BC) forced him to return to Asia. The Romans pursued him, and he was again defeated at the Battle of Magnesia (190 BC), forcing him to cede most of western Asia Minor to the Romans in return for peace. These defeats prompted the eastern provinces to rebel again, and Antiochus died in Persia while attempting to regain control of the province.

Below: Antiochus mourning the death of his stepmother, from in a 19th century romantic painting.

Ardashir I of Sassan
(reigned 226-241 BC)
King of Sassanid Persia

Ardashir deposed his brother and took the kingship of Fars, a small province of Persia, in 208 AD. He quickly expanded his territory by conquering neighboring provinces, but this aggression attracted the attention of Ardashir's overlord, Artabanus IV, ruler of the Parthian Empire. This led to conflict in 224 AD, which resulted in the death of Artabanus and allowed Ardashir to invade the western provinces of the Parthian Empire.

In 226 AD Ardashir was crowned ruler of Persia and took the title "king of kings." His reign brought to an end the 400-year-old Parthian empire and heralded the beginning of four centuries of Sassanid rule. Ardashir set about centralizing power and positioning loyal family members in the provinces. He also promoted Zoroastrianism as the state religion. Having secured his

Below: A youthful Sassanid nobleman, in a bas-relief celebrating King Ardashir of Persia.

Antiochus IV "Epiphanes"
(215-164 BC)
King of Seleucia

Following his accession, this son of Antiochus III conquered most of Ptolemaic Egypt, but was forced to withdraw when a Roman diplomat drew "a line in the sand," threatening war with Rome if crossed. Antiochus' aggressive policies also provoked the Revolt of the Maccabees in Judea.

Above: A damaged Roman bronze sculpture of Antiochus IV.

power base, in 230 AD Ardashir decided to tackle Persia's great rival in the west, the Roman Empire. He led his army into the Roman provinces of Mesopotamia and campaigned there, with limited success, for several years.

Ardashir died in 241 AD having successfully conducted a siege against the fortress of Hatra. Although he achieved only partial success against the Romans, he was able to deliver a more unified and powerful Persia to his son, Shapur I.

Below: Sassanid bas-relief carving from the necropolis of Naqsh-e Rustam in Iran, showing King Ardashir of Persia receiving a ribboned crown from the Persian God Ahura Mazda.

Ariovistus

**(c.58 BC), Chief of the Suebi,
Leader of the Germans**

Ariovistus was described as "king" and "friend" by the Roman Senate. His authority probably only extended to those Germans living in Gaul. In fact other tribes complained of his cruelty and pleaded with Caesar to intervene. Ariovistus refused a summons to appear before Caesar, not wanting to enter Roman territory without his army. He asserted his right to exact tribute from his neighbours and boasted of equal status with Rome. This was unacceptable to Caesar who began to mobilised his army.

As the two armies approached, the two leaders met each with an escort of their own cavalry, views were exchanged but no agreement was reached and the meeting came to an end when the German cavalry began to hurl missiles. Skirmishing developed between the two armies and Ariovistus managed to cut Caesar's supply line, isolating his camp. Caesar had to fight a battle or starve. He formed his legions and attacked but the Germans responded and drove back the Roman line, however when the Roman reserve was committed the Germans were themselves driven back, and with no reserve, broke.

Although Ariovistus escaped the battle he died shortly after. Ariovistus was a skillful general and Caesar found him not uncivilised, but he clearly miscalculated Roman tolerance for rivals.

Above: The defeat of Ariovistus by the Romans in 58 BC.

Arminius
**(18 BC-21 AD), Chief of the Cherusci,
Leader of the Germans**

Ashoka "the Great"
**(c.304-232 BC)
Indian Maurya Emperor**

A German leader who had spent time in the Roman Empire as a youth, he fully understood Rome's military methods – and how to counter them. Consequently when the Romans invaded German territory in 9 AD Arminius and his coalition of German tribes successfully defeated them at the Battle of the Teutoburg Forest.

Regarded as one of Indians greatest Emperors, Ashoka expanded the Maurya Empire through military conquest. One of these victories was won at the expense of the Republic of Kalinga, and reputedly Ashoka was so horrified by the suffering he caused that he converted to Buddhism, and devoted his last years to religious observance rather than to warfare.

Above: Arminius, the German tribal leader, depicted in a 19th century woodblock.

Above: The four lions back to back, shown in a copy of the sculpted Lion Capital of Ashoka.

Left: Annals of King Ashurbanipal, in the Louvre, Paris.
Above: Assyrian light infantry, in a bas-relief carving from the Palace of Siniveh, c.650 BC.
Right: Ashurbanipal in his chariot, in an Assyrian bas-relief carving from the Palace of Sennacherib at Nineveh, c.650 BC.

Ashurbanipal
(685-627 BC)
King of Assyria

Ashurbanipal succeeded to the throne on the death of his father Esarhaddon in 669BC. Much of his early career was taken up with campaigning, he put down a revolt in Egypt and captured Memphis in 668BC, he led a campaign against the Elam in 667BC and he sacked Thebes, having suppressed a second Egyptian revolt, in 663BC. In 658BC he captured Tyre and conquered much of Syria. Ashurbanipal then had to face a challenge from his brother Shamash-shuma-ukin who led a revolt in Babylonia in 652BC. This was eventually crushed when Babylon was captured after a two year siege. There were further campaigns against the Elam in 647-640BC which resulting in the sack of their capital at Susa.

The final decade of Ashurbanipal's reign was a period of relative peace in Assyria although the country was now in serious decline. Towards the end of his reign Ashurbanipal health began to fail and he was beset by scandal and intrigue. He died at Nineveh in 630 or 627.

Ashurbanipal was an energetic and resolute leader, however, the constant campaigning in the early years of his reign had weakened the Assyrian state which resulted in a power struggle after his death.

Attila
(406–453 AD)
King of the Huns

Attila "the Hun," the barbarian leader known as the "Scourge of God," was probably the most fearsome enemy the Romans ever faced. The Huns were a confederation of Eurasian tribes who lived in the steppes of Central Asia. In the late 4th century they began moving west, forcing the Goths to move westwards themselves in an effort to avoid being overwhelmed by the Asiatic invaders. By the early 5th century the leader of the Huns was King Ruglia, and on his death in 434 AD leadership passed to his two nephews, Attila and Bleda. The following year the pair negotiated at treaty with the envoys of the Eastern Roman Emperor Theodosius II, who paid the Huns to stay outside the Roman frontier.

This payment of protection money worked for about five years, largely because the Huns were occupied fighting the Sassanid Persians in the Middle East. However, in 440 AD the Huns reappeared on the borders of the Eastern Roman Empire, whose defenses had been stripped by the Emperor Theodosius. Attila and Bleda therefore crossed the Danube and began ravaging the Roman provinces of Moesia and

Right: Attila and his Huns receiving the surrender of the Roman city of Perugia in the early 5th century AD, in a 15th century painting by Benedetto Bonfigli.

ATTILA FLAGEL:DEI

Theodosius had little option but to negotiate another payment.

After their demands were met the Huns retired back across the Danube with their plunder. At that point Bleda died—Roman historians suggest that he was killed by his brother. Whatever happened, in 445 AD Attila became the sole and undisputed King of the Huns. Two years later he reappeared on the Danube, and in what is now Bulgaria defeated a Gothic army in Roman pay. Attila ravaged the Balkans a second time, his troops venturing as far south as the borders of Greece. Constantinople was protected by its walls, but all the Eastern Roman (or Byzantine) lands to the east were left at the mercy of the Huns. It was said that the dead could not be numbered, and the land was blighted. In 448 AD the hard-pressed Byzantines negotiated yet another treaty, and the Huns moved on.

While this was taking place Attila had successfully negotiated an alliance with Aetius, the military representative of the Western Roman Emperor Valentian III. He agreed to attack the Visigoths in what is now Southern France. However, the agreement foundered following the death of the Frankish king and the sibling power struggle that followed. Attila supported one royal brother, while Valentian and Aetius backed the other. To back his claimant Attila

Illyria (an area which now encompasses most of the Balkan States). They sacked Singidunum (now Belgrade) in 441 AD, then paused to regroup, and to demand more protection money. Theodosius refused, and recalled his troops to Constantinople (now Istanbul). Then in 443 AD the two Hun commanders struck again, capturing Serdica (Sofia), then driving the Roman army back to the walls of Constantinople.

Left: St. Genevieve, patron saint of Paris, driving the Hun from the city in 450 AD (from a 16th century painting).
Below: A 19th century depiction of Attila awed by the size and grandeur of Rome.

crossed the Rhine with his Huns, supported by allies drawn from numerous other barbarian tribes, including the Ostrogoths and the Alans. It was said that his army contained up to half a million warriors. In 451 AD Attila occupied Belgica (now Belgium), and in April he captured Metz. Aetius advanced to meet him, drawing support from the Franks and the Visigoths.

The two armies met near Chalons in the Marne, in a battle that, at least on paper, resulted in a decisive victory for Aetius. However, his Visigothic ally King Theodoric was killed in the battle, and the Roman alliance with the Visigoths collapsed. For his part Attila retreated back over the River Rhine, but the following year his army returned to the Roman Frontier, this time attacking northern Italy. The Huns rampaged through the area, destroying towns, and forcing many Italians to flee to the safety of the Venetian lagoon—a sanctuary that soon developed into the city of Venice.

Aetius lacked the strength to fight Attila, and could do little more than protect the Emperor Valentian, who had fled Ravenna to take sanctuary in Rome. However, his troops harassed the Huns, and prevented Attila from marching south in pursuit of the emperor. Pope Leo I met Attila in late 452 AD, and successfully negotiated a peace deal, whereby Attila would withdraw to the north in return for more ransom. Attila complied, and retired across the River Danube. That winter he planned to launch a new assault on Constantinople, but he died suddenly, possibly from choking to death during a banquet. Other sources claim Attila was assassinated by agents of the Byzantines.

Augustus (Gaius Julius Caesar Octavian)

(63 BC-AD 14), Republican Roman General, Statesmen, and First Roman Emperor

The young Gaius Octavius was born into a leading Roman family, although his father died when he was still an infant. When he was a teenager his great uncle Julius Caesar official adopted Octavian as his son. Following Caesar's assassination in 44 BC the nineteen-year-old Octavian inherited his estate, and rallied many of Caesar's veteran soldiers to his side. This made him a formidable political force, and so took the field against Mark Antony, who stood in opposition to both Caesar's assassins and to Octavian. However, when the Senate sided with the assassins Octavian formed an alliance, known as the Second

Triumvirate, with Antony and Marcus Aemilius Lepidus. Brutus, Cassius, and the other assassins fled to Greece, where they raised an army. Octavian and Antony pursued them, and in 42 BC they crushed their rivals at the Battle of Philippi.

In the peace that followed, Antony ruled the Eastern Provinces from Egypt, Lepidus took control of Africa and Spain, while Octavian administered Italy and Rome. However, the Triumvirate was soon torn apart by political rivalry when Antony provoked rebellion in Italy. However, in 40 BC a new alliance was agreed, and a semblance of peace was maintained. Four years later Lepidus tried to wrest control of Sicily from Octavian, but his troops deserted him, and Lepidus was exiled. This left

Right: A bronze statue of Augustus, the first Roman Emperor, from Turin, Italy. The successful Roman general Octavian assumed the title in 27 BC.
Below: A Roman silver coin, carrying the head of the Emperor Augustus, 1st century AD.

Above: Emperor Augustus and his family, in a Roman bas-relief dating from the early 1st century AD.

Above right: The ruins of the temple of Augustus in Rome, built by the Emperor Tiberius to honor Augustus, his adoptive father.

Left: Augustus Octavian's foe, Mark Antony, is brought dying to Cleopatra, (from a painting by 19th century French artist Ernest Hillemacher).

Octavian and Antony in control of the Roman world.

A showdown was inevitable, and so in 32 BC Octavian declared war on Antony and his mistress, Queen Cleopatra of Egypt. The two forces met at sea off Actium (31 BC), where Octavian's fleet was commanded by his able subordinate Agrippa. The battle ended in a stunning victory for Octavian, who pursued the lovers to Alexandria. Rather than face Octavian they both committed suicide. On paper Octavian maintained the façade of the Roman Republic, but in practice he retained his autocratic power. It took several years for the nature of this power to develop, but in 27 BC the Republic was dissolved and Octavian became Rome's first emperor. He adopted the name Augustus, and ruled his empire successfully until his death. During his reign the borders of the Roman Empire were consolidated, and Rome prospered. On his death he was succeeded as emperor by his adoptive son Tiberius.

Aulus Plautius

(c.43-60 AD)
Imperial Roman General and Statesman

Plautius commanded the Roman army that invaded Britain in 43 AD, conquering the southern portion of the country in a lightning campaign. For the next four years he served as the governor of the newly conquered province, ensuring it remained firmly under Roman control.

Aurelian
(Lucius Domitius Aurelianus)

(214-275 AD, reigned 270-275 AD)
Roman General and Emperor

Born into a humble family, Aurelian took his name from the senator Aurelius whom his family served. He rose quickly through the ranks of the army, becoming a cavalry commander in the army of the Emperor Gallienus, At the Battle of Naissus in 268 AD his cavalry broke the formidable cavalry of the Goths. Following the death of the Emperor Claudius, Aurelian was proclaimed emperor by his own troops, and was eventually recognized by the Senate.

In 270 AD, Aurelian drove out the Vandals and Sarmatians who were threatening Italia. In the following year he faced a new threat from the Alamanni and although his forces were initially defeated he managed to break the invaders at Pavia. By 272 AD Aurelian had regained the lost eastern provinces of the empire—Syria, Palestine, and Egypt, ruled by Queen Zenobia. In 275 AD Aurelian marched towards Asia Minor but was murdered in Thrace by officers of the Praetorian Guard who had been led to expect severe punishment from the emperor.

Aurelian was a highly successful emperor; responsible for restoring many public buildings and instigating important religious reforms. His military success enabled him to reunite the empire and restore security to its frontiers for the next 200 years.

Left: The Aurelian Walls, built in 3rd century AD around all seven hills of Rome.
Below: The Emperor Aurelian (reigned 270-275 AD), on a late 3rd century AD Roman coin.

Bahram V of Persia (or Bahramgur)
(reigned 421-476 AD)
King of Sassanid Persia

Bahram began his reign by fighting an inconclusive war with the Eastern Roman Empire, but a peace treaty was eventually concluded. Then, when faced with invasion by the Huns, Bahram launched a surprise attack that drove the invaders from Persia.

Above: Bahram V ("Bahram Gur"), King of Sassanid Persia, hunting with his mistress (from a 16th century Turkish manuscript).

Basiliscus

(reigned 475-476 AD)
Roman General & Eastern Roman Emperor

In 468 AD the Eastern Roman General Basiliscus launched an unsuccessful amphibious invasion of Vandal North Africa. Seven years later he seized control of the Eastern Roman Empire in a coup. The Emperor Zeno reclaimed his throne the following year, and Basiliscus was duly executed.

Left: The Eastern Roman Emperor Basiliscus, shown in this 5th century AD Byzantine ivory panel accompanied by his wife, Aelia Zenonis.

Boudica

(died 61 AD)
Queen of the Iceni, British Leader

Boudica (also spelled Boudicca) was queen of the Iceni tribe and ruled the peoples of Eastern England with her husband, King Prasutagus. The Iceni had been a client kingdom of Rome since the invasion of England in AD 43. However, when the king died in AD 60 the Romans decided to rule directly. The Iceni chiefs found their property confiscated and their people enslaved, Boudica was stripped and flogged and her daughters were raped, a final act of humiliation that further inflamed opposition to Roman rule.

In AD 61 this opposition broke out into open rebellion led by Boudica and the Iceni tribe. Their first target was Camulodunum (Colchester), a Roman settlement that they destroyed and where they put to flight a Roman Legion. The Roman governor, Gaius Suetonius Paulinus, decided that his force was not strong enough to defend the area and withdrew to the West Midlands where he would make a

Right: Boudica, Queen of the Iceni, in a romanticized early 19th century portrait.

Boadicea, Queen of the Iceni.

Published June 1, 1825 by R. Havell, 3. Chapel Street, London.

Above: Warrior Queen Boudica on her chariot, in a statue in front of the Houses of Parliament, London.

stand. In the wake of the Roman withdrawal, the rebels destroyed Londinium (London) and Verulamium (St. Albans), slaughtering around 80,000 inhabitants.

By the time Boudica's rebel force moved north to face the Roman army it was an estimated 230,000 strong, twenty times larger than the Roman army. However, Boudica's force lacked the discipline of the well-trained Roman soldiers and this led to its downfall. When the two armies met, in a narrow wooded defile near Watling Street, Boudica could not make use of her superior numbers and the ordered ranks of Roman soldiers slaughtered the rebels. According to Tacitus, the Roman army lost 400 men, but 80,000 Britons were killed that day. Boudica escaped death in battle, but died later from taking poison or perhaps from a sickness. Whatever her fate, the rebellion was over and the resistance of the tribes had been crushed.

Described as a tall woman with long red hair and a piercing gaze, Boudica exhorted her troops from her chariot and fought and died for the freedom of the tribes. Her rebellion was the only serious challenge to Roman rule in Britain until the fifth century and two millennia later Boudica remains one of Britain's greatest heroines.

Brasidas
(c.424 BC)
Spartan General

Brasidas campaigned in Thrace against the Athenians and was briefly allied with Perdiccas of Macedonia. He was killed at Amphipolis, having routed an Athenian force. Brasidas possessed all of the bravery expected of a Spartan officer but was also a skilled and decisive tactician, and an appealing orator.

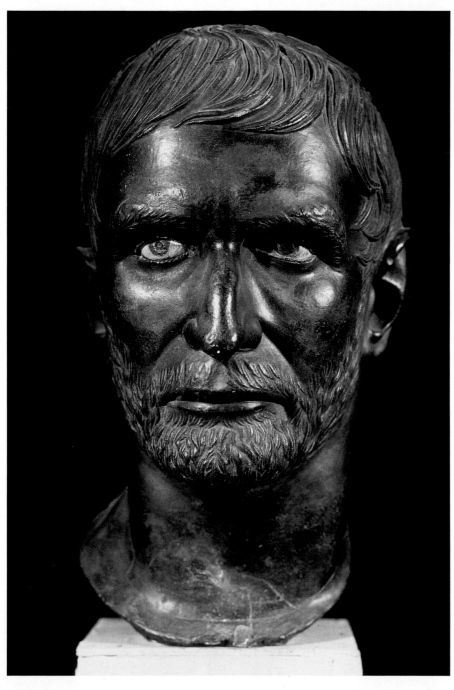

Marcus Junius Brutus
(85-42 BC), Republican Roman General and Statesman

Brutus fought during the civil war at the Battle of Pharsalus in 49 BC. Caesar appointed him governor of Gaul, but Brutus became one of the assassins who murdered Caesar in 44 BC. Octavian declared the murderers enemies of the state and Brutus was eventually defeated at the Second Battle of Philippi in 42 BC, after which he committed suicide.

Left: A bronze bust of Marcus Brutus, the adoptive son and the assassin of Julius Caesar, from the Museo della Civilta, Rome.

Calgacus
(c.83 AD)
Chief of the Caledonians

The leader of the Caledonii who opposed the invasion of Scotland by Agricola in 81 AD, Calgacus was finally defeated at the Battle of Mons Graupius in 84 AD. He is best remembered for the stirring pre-battle speech credited to him by the Roman historian Tacitus.

Cao Cao
(155-220 AD)
Chinese Han Warlord

Caracalla
(reigned 198-217 AD)
Roman Emperor and General]

A warlord who rose to power during the last decades of the Han dynasty, Cao Cao became the ruler of Wei, one of the principal Chinese states of the Three Kingdoms Era. He won a notable military victory at the Battle of Guandu (200 AD), but suffered defeat at the Battle of Red Cliffs (208 BC), both battles being fought against rival warlords.

Above: A 16th century Chinese depiction of the 3rd century Warlord Cao Cao and his commanders, on the banks of the Yangtze River.

After succeeding his father Septimus Severus, Caracalla led expeditions across the German frontier, but despite his popularity in the army he was regarded as a tyrannical ruler. He was eventually assassinated while preparing to launch a campaign against the Parthians.

Above: A marble bust of Caracalla, renowned as being one of the most psychotic of all the Roman Emperors.

Above: A poster showing the 18th century actor Mr. Butler playing the part of Caratacus, with an Ancient British druidic ceremony supposedly being performed in the background.

Caratacus
(c.80 AD)
Chieftain of the Catuvellauni

Caratacus led his people, the British Catuvellauni, to victory against their rivals, the Atrebates under Verica. The latter fled to Rome and appealed to the Emperor Claudius for help, which was granted and resulted in the Roman invasion of Britain in 43 AD.

With his brother Togodumnus, Caratacus led the resistance against the invasion by using their familiarity with the terrain to employ irregular tactics but the defenders were defeated in the crucial battles of Medway and Thames. The Catuvellauni's territories were conquered and Togodumnus was killed, but Caratacus managed to escape and continued to organize resistance. Eventually, in 51 AD Caratacus was defeated and his wife and daughters were captured. Once again Caratacus escaped and but was handed over in chains by the Brigantes who were loyal to Rome.

Following his capture, Caratacus was sent to Rome to be displayed as a war prize during a triumphal parade. Although still a prisoner, he was allowed to speak to the Roman Senate, and Tacitus records how well his speech was received. In fact, so great was the impression he made that he received a full pardon and was allowed to live in peace in Rome.

Carausius
(reigned 286-295 AD)
Roman Emperor

In 286 AD Marcus Aurelius Carausius was the experienced commander of the Roman fleet in Britain. Later that year he declared himself Emperor of Britain and Northern Gaul, and thus a rival to the Emperor Maximian. His revolt lasted for thirteen years, until Carausius was assassinated by one of his advisors.

Marcus Aurelius Carus
(d. 283 AD)
Roman Emperor

A capable and successful general, Carus is thought to have been born in 225 AD in southern Gaul. Little is known of Carus's early career. He was employed in several military and civil posts, eventually becoming proconsul of Cilicia. In 282 AD he was proclaimed emperor by the upper

Danube legions in Raetia and Noricum following the death of Probus, despite suspicions of having had a hand in the emperor's murder.

Before embarking on his first major campaign, Carus conferred the title of Caesar on his sons. He left his eldest son Carinus in charge in the West and led his army east with his younger son Numerianus. In a campaign along the Danube he defeated the Sarmatians and the Quadi. He then headed for Asia Minor where he crossed the Tigris River and overcame the Persians at Ctesiphon in 283 AD. Having captured Ctesiphon and Seleucia he died suddenly. His death has been variously attributed to disease, plague, wounds, or even the effects of lightning. It is even possible that he was assassinated. However, the peaceful succession by his son Numerian suggests that he died of natural causes.

Left: Marcus Aurelius Carus portrayed on a Roman silver coin dating from the late 3rd century AD.
Below: Roman hero Marcus Aurelius Carus, depicted on a posthumous coin.

Cassander
(350-297 BC, ruled 305-297)
Macedonian General and King

One of the Macedonian "Successor Generals," Cassander allied himself with Ptolemy "Soter," then campaigned against the armies led by Olympias, mother of Alexander the Great, and eventually seized control of Macedonia. He held the kingdom against his rival Antigonus, but died before he could campaign against his other rival "successors".

Cassivellannus
(c.54 BC)
British Chief of the Catuvellauni

Cassivellaunus led the British forces against Julius Caesar's second expedition to Britain in 54 BC, mainly using irregular tactics to disrupt Roman foraging and patrols. His stronghold was besieged and the Roman force managed to beat off a relief force of Kentish chiefs. Cassivellaunus surrendered and swore not to resume hostilities against the Romans.

Chanakya
(c. 350-283 BC)
Indian Statesman & Author

Although not a military leader per se, Chanakya was the political advisor of Chandragupta, India's first Maurya Emperor. He was also most probably the author of the *Artha?h?stra*, a guide to military strategy and statecraft that is comparable with the works of Sun Tsu and Machiavelli.

Chandragupta (or Chandragupta Maurya)

(c.340-293 BC), Indian Maurya Emperor

The founder of the Maurya Empire, Chandragupta carved out his own kingdom in the basin of the River Ganges, and by defeating Seleucus Nicator he safeguarded the northern borders of modern India. Today he is seen as the first unifier in Indian history.

Chandragupta II (also Vikramaditya)

(ruled 375-415 AD)), Indian Gupta King

One of the most powerful Emperors of the Gupta dynasty, Chandragupta II pursued an aggressive policy of expansionism, his most notable conquest being over his brother, Rudrasimha II, ruler of Gujarat. By the time of his death his realm covered all of Northern India.

Cleon

(d.422 BC)
Athenian General & Statesman

An aristocrat and politician, Cleon became the most prominent man in Athens. A powerful and eloquent speaker, he hated Sparta and captured an Athenian force stranded on the island of Sphacteria. Cleon was sent to relieve Amphipolis but was defeated by Brasidas and died during the battle that allowed peace to be concluded the following year.

Constantine I (Flavius Valerius Aurelius Constantinus)

(272-337 AD, reigned 306-337 AD), Roman Emperor

Constantine was born in the city of Naissus around 272 AD; he was the son of Flavius Constantius, who would later become emperor. In his early career Constantine fought in Asia, Persia, and along the Danube. In 306 AD, following

Below: The marble head of the Emperor Constantine "the Great," designed as part of an enormous statue that was never erected.

Above: The Arch of Constantine was built as a triumphal monument, designed to commemorate Constantine's victory over his rival Maxentius in 315 AD.

the death of his father, he was proclaimed Emperor of the West, which included Britain, Gaul, Germania, and Hispania.

At the Battle of Milvian Bridge in 312 AD, Constantine dreamt that the Christian God promised him victory if his soldiers carried an image of the Cross on their shields. In the following year Constantine and Licinius, Emperor of the Eastern Empire, signed the Edict of Milan, which allowed for full toleration of the Christian religion.

In 324 AD, Constantine conquered the Eastern Empire during the civil war against Licinius. In 325 AD, in an attempt to gain consensus across the entire Christian world, Constantine summoned the Council of Nicaea, which resulted in the first uniform Christian doctrine. Five years later, Constantine founded the city of Constantinople as capital of Eastern Empire.

Constantine died in 337 AD and was baptized on his deathbed. Although many have doubted the authenticity of his conversion he is still remembered as being the first Christian emperor, responsible for reuniting both halves of the empire and establishing Christianity as its primary religion.

Below: A detail from the Arch of Constantine, showing the Emperor Constantine receiving the adulation of his soldiers after his victory at the Battle of the Milvian Bridge, 312 AD.

Constantius II
(317-361 AD, reigned 337-361 AD)
Roman Emperor

Following the death of Constantine I "the Great" in 337 AD the Empire was divided between his three sons. Constantius acquired control of the Eastern Empire, but in 350 AD he was faced with a usurper, Magnantius. Constantius defeated his rival at the Battle of Mursa Major (351 AD), and so regained control over his Empire.

Above: The Emperor Constantius II, from a mid 5th century Roman gold coin found in Antioch.

Above: Crassus ransacks the Temple of Jerusalem, from a painting by Giovanni Battista Pittoni, 1743.

Left: A marble bust of Marcus Crassus, the third and least successful member of the "Triumvirate."

Marcus Lucinius Crassus

(115-53 BC)
Republican Roman General and Statesman

Crassus was born into a wealthy Roman family, the son of a consul who was killed during the Marian purges in 87 BC. He distinguished himself at the Battle of Colline Gate in 82 BC and became one of the richest men in Rome, gaining great wealth through slave trafficking and the purchase of estates of men proscribed by the dictator Sulla.

He used his wealth to gain influence, promoting the career of the young Julius Caesar, and in 73 BC he was elected praetor.

Although Crassus experienced military success with his crushing of the slave revolt of Spartacus in 70 BC he was nonetheless jealous of the military achievements of his rivals. In 54 BC he appointed himself proconsul for Syria and launched an ill-judged invasion of Parthia. This led to defeat at Carrhae and his death in its aftermath (53 BC). According to legend, Crassus was killed by having molten gold poured down his throat to finally quench his thirst for wealth, although this is likely to have been a rumor spread by his many Roman enemies.

Undoubtedly a skilful politician, Crassus is better known for his avarice. His military skills may have won him success against Spartacus but they were not sufficient to defeat the Parthians.

Cyrus "the Great"
(c.590-530 BC)
King of Babylonia

Darius "the Great"
(c.549-485 BC)
King of Persia

Cyrus united the Persians and Medes into a single empire; he fought against the Median, Lydian, and Neo-Babylonian empires. Cyrus tolerated religions in newly conquered regions, which gained him valuable support, and the political infrastructure he developed meant that his Archaemenid empire continued long after his death.

Darius faced many revolts during his reign in Babylonia and Greece. He introduced a number of military reforms including conscription and pay for soldiers. Darius was responsible for a huge building program, including a new capital at Persepolis, He developed commerce and expanded trade, standardized weights and measures, and extended considerable religious toleration to his subjects.

Above: The simple mausoleum of King Cyrus "the Great" of Persia, in Pasargade, Iran.

Above: Darius "the Great," King of Persia, from a 5th century BC bas-relief carving from Persepolis, Iran.

Darius III
(380-330 BC)
King of Persia

Decebalus
(reigned 86-106 AD)
King of Dacia

Darius inherited a dangerously unstable empire that was invaded by Philip II and then Alexander the Great. He suffered a series of defeats against Alexander, at Granicus in 334 BC, at Issus 333 BC, and finally at Gaugamela in 331 BC, from where Darius fled to Ecbatana to raise another army but was murdered soon after.

Above: King Darius in his chariot, confronted by Alexander the Great at the Battle of Issus, from a Roman mosaic dating from the 2nd-1st century BC, from the House of the Faun, Pompeii.

Dacia lay beyond the Danube frontier of the Roman Empire, a kingdom that encompassed much of modern Romania. The kingdom had once been united, but by the mid 1st century BC it had fragmented into several smaller states. The ruler of one of these was known as Diurpaneus, whose capital was Sarmizegetusa, a mountain stronghold east of the modern city of Timi?oara. By 85 AD another ruler—Duras—had managed to weld these states into a kingdom again, and he began launching raids into Roman

territory across the River Danube. The Emperor Domitian ordered his legions to retaliate, and so in 87 AD his commander Cornelius Fuscus led a punitive expedition of some 25,000 men into Dacia. The Roman column was ambushed at Tapae by Diurpaneus, whose Dacians wiped out two Roman legions and killed their commander. Following the victory the Dacian general changed his name to Decebalus (meaning "the brave"), and replaced Duras as king.

The Romans returned the following year, but after some initial success the invasion ground to a halt, as incursions elsewhere in the Empire meant that troops had to be diverted from Dacia. Consequently, a peace was concluded, although both sides realized that there was still unfinished business to settle. This peace lasted until the accession of the Emperor Trajan (98 AD), who made preparations for a renewal of the war. In 101 AD Trajan's engineers bridged

Above: The Dacian army led by King Decebalus taking refuge from the Romans, in a detail from Trajan's Column, early 2nd century AD.

the Danube and the emperor personally led his legions northwards towards Sarmizegetusa. The following year Trajan and Decebalus clashed at the Second Battle of Tapae, and this time it was the Dacians who were vanquished.

Trajan went into winter quarters,

planning to renew the offensive the following spring, but Decebalus had other plans. He raided across the Danube, and at the Battle of Adamclisi (102 AD) he destroyed a Roman legion sent in pursuit of him. The Dacian king enjoyed a reprieve when Trajan returned to Rome, but the ceasefire that followed came to an end three years later. In 105 AD the Romans laid siege to Sarmizegetusa, which fell early the following year. Decebalus elected to take his own life rather than be captured by the Romans.

Demetrius I "Poliocetes"
(336-283 BC)
King of Macedon

Below: A reconstruction of the siege tower used by Demetrius "Poliorcetes" during the Siege of Rhodes, 305 BC.

Demetrius was born the son of Antigonus I (Alexander the Great's general). Although he was defeated at Gaza (312 BC) he found success in 307 BC when he gained control of much of Greece. His reputation was further enhanced when he besieged the city of Rhodes (305-304 BC) with great skill, during which he earned his cognomen Poliocetes ("Besieger of Cities").

Summoned to Asia by his father to join him on campaign, he suffered defeat at Ipsus in 301 BC in a battle that also resulted in the death of his father. With only a small fleet, Demetrius managed to regain much of his father's territory, retaking Athens in 294 BC and declaring himself king of Macedon. Demetrius gradually established control over Greece and drove Pyrrhus and Lysimachus out of Macadon in 288 BC. He went on to invade Asia Minor with a small mercenary army but, detached from his fleet, he was deserted by his troops and surrendered to Seleucus in Cilicia in 285 BC. Demetrius died in captivity in 283 BC.

Demetrius was a competent and resolute soldier but he tended to be reckless without his father's influence. Despite his eventual defeat his descendants remained in possession of the Macedonian throne for another eighty years until Macedon was conquered by the Romans in 168 BC.

Demetrius I (the Invincible)
(reigned c. 200-180 BC)
King of Bactria

The son of Euthydemus, Demetrius began his reign in 200 BC. He conquered large areas of what is now Afghanistan, Iran, and Pakistan, creating an Indo-Greek kingdom far from Hellenistic Greece. He was never defeated in battle and was honored with the title "invincible" after his death.

Demosthenes
(384-322 BC)
Athenian Statesman and Strategist

Diocletian (Gaius Aurelius Valerius Diocletianus)
(236-316 AD, reigned 284-305 AD)
Roman General and Emperor

For more than two decades the Athenian statesman Demosthenes organized Greek political and military opposition to the expansionist policies of Philip II of Macedon. At the climactic Battle of Chaeronea (338 BC) he fought among the Athenian hoplites, and continued to oppose the Macedonians until his death.

Above: A marble bust of the gifted Athenian statesman Dimosthenes, who opposed Macedonian domination of the Greek City States.

Born to humble parents in Dalmatia, Diocletian joined the army and rose to command Emperor Numerian's bodyguard. He was elected emperor following Numerian's murder in 284 AD and promptly killed the alleged assassin,

Above: A late 3rd century marble bust of the Emperor Diocletian, now in the Archaeological Museum of Istanbul.
Following page: Gladiators fighting wild animals in the gladiatorial arena, from a Roman mosaic of the 2nd or early 3rd century AD.

Aper. Diocletian then led an army against Numerian's brother Carinus and defeated him in battle in southeastern Illyicum in 285 AD. In an attempt to extend his power and so reduce the potential for further military coups, Diocletian appointed his friend Maximian Caesar as assistant emperor. Later he appointed two new Caesars, Gaius Valerius Galerius and Flavius Valerius, the Tetrarchy, in 286 AD.

Diocletian went on to expand the size of the army and managed to restore a certain amount of peace and prosperity to the empire. He reorganized imperial administration into civil and military authorities and in 296 AD created smaller provinces, grouping them into twelve larger districts called dioceses. Later that year Diocletian suppressed the revolt of Domitius Domitianus in Egypt. Eventually, Diocletian retired to his palace in Dalmatia and died in retirement in 312 or 313 AD.

Although Diocletian drastically reformed the late Roman Empire, the Tetrarch system did eventually collapse into civil war. His greatest measure of success,

however, is that he ruled for twenty-one years and retired voluntarily, a feat that few other emperors achieved.

Above: St. George appearing before the Roman Emperor Diocletian, from a 13th century Italian manuscript celebrating the life of the saint.

Left: The Tetrarchs—Diocletian's four rulers of the Empire—from a Byzantine statue sculpted in porphyry rock during the early 4th century AD, and now displayed in Venice.

Dionysus I
(c.432-367 BC)
Tyrant of Syracuse

Regarded by his contemporaries as a malicious and merciless tyrant, Dionysus started his career as a humble clerk but rose to command the army in 406 BC after his successes in the war against Carthage. Following this he seized total power and brutally consolidated his position. Accounts of his death vary from natural causes to poisoning.

Domitian (Titus Flavius Domitianus)
(51-96 AD), Roman Emperor

The second son of Vespasian and Flavia Domitilla, Domitian was forced to hide from his father's enemies during the civil war of 68 to 69 AD. Later he became consul under Vespasian. In 79 AD Vespasian died and was succeeded by Titus, whose short reign ended in his death in 81 AD. Titus was succeeded by Domitian who was declared emperor by the Praetorian Guard.

Domitian retained close control over the magistrates and provinces and led repeated campaigns against barbarians along the Rhine and Danube rivers. In 88 AD he routed the Dacians at Tapae and subdued the Sarmatians in 92 AD. Despite these victories he was unable to stabilize the frontiers and endured a revolt by the governor of Upper Germany, Antonius Aturninus, in 89 AD. Further unrest caused him to deal harshly with political opponents; at least twenty of his political rivals were executed, including his cousin, the Consul Flavius Clemens. This reign of terror was brought to an end with Domitian's murder in Rome by a group of conspirators which included his wife in 96AD.

Although often regarded as a cruel and insecure tyrant, Domitian was also an able and energetic soldier and administrator; however, it was his former qualities that were most evident at the end of his reign.

Above: A marble bust of the Emperor Domitian dating from the late 1st century AD, and now in the Museo Capitolino, Rome.
Right: The Emperor Domitian, as portrayed on a Roman bronze coin dating from the late 1st century AD.

Epaminondas
(418–362 BC)
Theban General and Statesman

As a statesman, Epaminondas master-minded the growth of Thebes as a Greek power during the 4th century BC, and as a general he led her army to victory against the Spartans at the Battle of Leuctra (371 BC), an engagement that ended Sparta's military dominance in Greece.

Left: The agora (an open "place of assembly") in the ancient city of Sparta, from whose subjugation Epaminondas led the city-state Thebes into a preeminent position in Greek politics.

Eurybiades
(c. 480 BC)
Spartan General

The commander of the Greek navy during the Persian Wars, Eurybiades led the fleet at the inconclusive Battle of Artimisium in 480 BC, and again at the Battle of Salamis. This battle resulted in the destruction of 200 Persian ships and was a decisive victory for the Greek fleet.

Left: A 16th century fresco depicts the Greek fleet under Eurybiades in one of many clashes with the Persian fleet in 480 BC.

Flavius Aetius
(396-454 AD)
Late Roman General

Aëtius saw early military service in the Western Empire and Africa and spent some time as a hostage to the Huns, among whom he made friends and managed to learn valuable military skills. In 425 AD he moved to support his ally Joannes, who had proclaimed himself emperor, but he arrived too late to prevent Joannes' defeat and execution.

Having received a pardon from Galla Placidia, the mother of Emperor Valentian III, Aëtius defeated Theodoric, the Visigoth king of Toulouse, in 425 AD. He followed this by re-establishing Roman control over much of Gaul (426-430 AD). Suspected of having imperial ambitions, Aëtius invaded Italy in 432 AD but was defeated near Ravenna by Boniface, who was killed in the battle. In 451 AD Aëtius assembled a coalition against Attila made up of Visigoths, Alans, and Burgundians. Attila's invasion of Gaul was halted at the battle of Châlons, and Attila was driven back across the Rhine.

Jealous of his success and suspecting that Aëtius wanted to put his own son on the imperial throne, the Emperor Valentian III murdered Aëtius in 453 AD. The following year Valentian was himself murdered by supporters of Aëtius while his guards looked on.

A bold and able Roman general, Aëtius is renowned for destroying Attila's reputation for invincibility.

Above: A less than flattering marble bust of Magnentius, an Imperial rival and usurper in the mid 4th century AD.

that of Magnentius at the Battle of Musra Major. The defeated usurper committed suicide two years later.

Flavius Magnus Magnentius
(303-353AD)
Roman General & Imperial usurper

A former commander of the Imperial Guard, in 350 AD Magnentius was proclaimed emperor by the Roman Army in the West, and successfully ousted the Emperor Constans from the throne. However, Constans' brother Constantius II still ruled in the East, and in 351 ADh is army defeated

Gaiseric (or Geiseric, Genseric)
(c.389-477 AD)
King of the Vandals

After being elected King of the Vandals in 428 AD, Gaiseric "the Lame" ferried his people from Spain over to Africa to carve out a secure homeland there at the expense of the Western Roman Empire. In 439 AD he captured Carthage, then used his fleet to dominate the Western Mediterranean.

Galba
(3 BC-69 AD
Roman Emperor

Germanicus Julius Caesar
(16 BC-19 AD)
Imperial Roman General

Galba was a consul by the age of thirty-three and served with distinction in Gaul, Hispania, and Germania. Although encouraged by his friends to make a bid for the empire he served Claudius faithfully. After Nero's death Galba took the title Caesar and marched on Rome. Galba was murdered following a revolt against unpopular measures to restore the empire's finances.

Above: Galba managed to remain Roman Emperor for only seven months during 69 AD, the Year of the Four Emperors

Above: A marble bust of the Emperor Germanicus, the adopted son of Tiberius, and a successful general in his own right.
Right: *The Death of Germanicus,* by 17th century artist Gerard de Lairesse.

Germanicus was the father of the Roman Emperor Caligula and grandfather of the Emperor Nero. He was appointed commander of the forces in Germania, and he led his troops on a raid into the upper Ruhr River, devastating wide areas. Germanicus launched a second invasion in 16

AD and met the army of Arminius at the Weser River. The better trained and equipped Romans inflicted huge losses on the German tribes. Further raids were carried out across the Rhine, resulting in the recovery of two eagles lost during the disastrous defeat in the Teutoburg Forest in 9 AD.

Following his successes, Germanicus was recalled to Rome and informed by Tiberius that he would be given a triumph, a move designed also to reign in his independent activities so far from Rome. In 18 AD Germanicus was sent to Asia where he conquered several provinces, but he died suddenly in Antioch in uncertain circumstances—possibly by poison. The suspicious death affected the popularity of the Emperor Tiberius and many feared the beginnings of tyrannical rule.

Germanicus had immense popularity among the citizens of Rome and for many he was the embodiment of Roman virtue. His death was seen as the decline of such virtue in an increasingly corrupt world.

Below: The Arch of Germanicus, built in the early 1st century AD in Saintes, near Charente, France.

Gnan Yu
(160-219 AD)
Chinese Shu Han General

A highly respected general who served the warlord Liu Bei, founder of the Shu Han dynasty, Guan Yu played a significant military role in the establishment of the Kingdom of Shu, and today he is venerated as a religious figure, the epitome of loyalty, morality, and chivalric virtue.

Above: The Chinese general Gnan Yu depicted playing a board game with his senior advisors.

Hadrian (Publius Aelius Traianus Hadrianus)

(76–138AD, reigned 117–138 AD)
Roman General and Emperor

Hadrian was born in Iberia in 76 AD and raised by his cousin, the future emperor Trajan. Hadrian saw action in the Dacian wars and was appointed governor of Syria in

Above: A marble bust of the Emperor Hadrian, an experienced military commander.
Right: A marble statue of Antinous, a close friend and favorite of the Emperor Hadrian, sculpted to resemble the Greek god Aristaeus.

Above: Hadrian's Wall at Crag Lough, Northumberland, northeast England.

114 AD. In 117 AD he was adopted by Trajan on his deathbed, and with senate approval became emperor. Hadrian quickly moved to suppress a conspiracy of four of Trajan's generals.

The emperor spent half his reign outside of Italy and traveled the provinces of the west in 121-123 AD, the east in 123-125 AD, and Africa in 128 AD. During his travels he ordered the construction of the defensive wall in across northern Britain and other defensive works in Germany along the Danube. In 130 AD, Hadrian visited the ruins of Jerusalem and made plans to rebuild the city and site a temple dedicated to Jupiter there. This triggered the Jewish uprising led by Bar Kokhba from 132 to 135 AD. The ensuing conflict resulted in huge Roman losses but the rebellion was eventually crushed, although Hadrian continued to persecute Judaism as he considered it a source of future unrest.

Hadrian died near Naples in 138 AD. He was a vigorous and efficient ruler but never particularly popular. However, Hadrian's extensive travels made him highly visible in the provinces and helped focus imperial authority in the emperor's person.

Hamilcar Barca
(270–228BC)
Carthaginian General

Hamilcar fought in the First Punic War in 247 BC and commanded a small mercenary force that attacked Roman positions in Sicily. He remained on the island until peace was concluded in 241 BC, when he returned to Carthage with his undefeated army.

In Carthage, mutiny broke out among Hamilcar's once loyal troops when promised rewards were withheld. This was a serious threat to Carthage, already weakened by war with Rome, but Hamilcar managed to win round some of the rebels and destroyed the rest in battle in 239 BC. Such was the extent of the victory and the esteem of the people that Hamilcar was awarded dictatorship over Carthage.

Hamilcar went on to develop a new army and set out to invade Hispania, which he hoped would compensate for the loss of Sicily and would provide a useful base from which to launch further attacks against Rome. After eight years of fighting and diplomatic maneuvering, Hamilcar had made significant gains, but his death in battle in 228 BC prevented him from completing the conquest.

Hamilcar possessed great military and diplomatic skills and an intense hatred of Rome, qualities that he passed on to his son Hannibal, who used them to even greater effect.

Above: Hamilcar Barca, as portrayed on a Punic coin, minted in Carthage around 230 BC.

Hammurabi
(c 1810–1750 BC)
King of Babylon

Han Xin
(c.240-196 BC)
Chinese Han General

The first king of the Babylonian Empire, Hammurabi conquered large areas of Mesopotamia. He devised the renowned Hammurabi Code, one of the first set of laws written in recorded history. His empire was not maintained after his death, although his laws were adopted by the Kassites who ruled Mesopotamia for 400 years.

Above: The head of Hamurabi, King of Babylon, carved in the 18th century BC, from Susa in Mesopotamia.

As a general in the service of the Han Emperor Gaozu, Han Xin guided his master to victory over his Chinese rivals. His most notable success was achieved at the Battle of the Tao River (205 BC), although his strategic destruction of the Quin dynasty was regarded as one of the most successful operations in Chinese military history.

Above: Legend has it that when Han Xin became successful he sought out an old lady who helped him as a youth, and thanked her for her kindness.

Hannibal
(247-188BC)
Carthaginian General

Hannibal, son of Hamilcar Barca, is generally regarded as Rome's greatest enemy, and one of the most formidable military commanders in history. His father campaigned extensively in what is now Spain, establishing Carthaginian provinces there and restoring the fortunes of his home state, which had suffered defeat at the hands of the Romans during the First Punic War. It is claimed that Hamilcar made his son swear an oath that as long as he lived Hannibal would never be a friend of Rome. His son remained true to his word.

When Hamilcar Barca was killed in battle in 228 BC his son-in-law Hasdrubal assumed command of the army in Spain until his assassination in 221 BC. The twenty-six-year-old Hannibal then assumed control of the Carthaginian army and then spent the next two years completing the pacification of Spain south of the Ebro River. The Romans began to become concerned about Hannibal, and in 219 BC they formed an alliance with the Spanish city of Saguntum, which lay deep inside Carthaginian territory. Hannibal besieged and captured the city, an act that the Romans claimed was tantamount to a declaration of

Below: *"Snowstorm: Hannibal crossing the Alps,"* a painting by J. M. W. Turner, and displayed in the Tate Gallery, London.

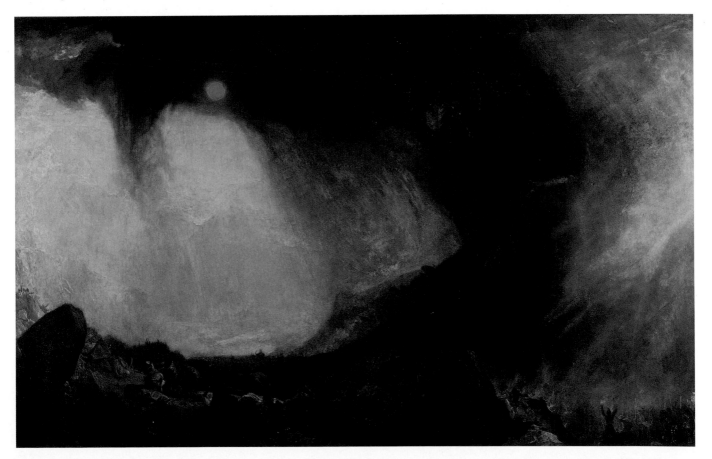

war. With war inevitable, Hannibal made preparations to lead his army into Italy, bringing the fight directly to the enemy.

What followed became known as the Second Punic War (218-203 BC). Between Hannibal and Italy lay the mountain ranges of the Pyrenees and the Alps, and the potentially hostile region of southern Gaul, where the coastal city of Massilia (now Marseilles) was allied to Rome. In the late spring of 218 BC Hannibal led his army across the river Ebro and into the Pyrenees, where he subdued the local tribes before continuing on into Gaul. By mid-summer he was across the River Rhône, having placated the Gallic local chiefs and evaded the Roman army sent from Massilia to intercept him. He then had to cross the Alps. His exact route is not known, but what is certain is that Hannibal's crossing of the Alps that fall with 46,000 men and thirty-seven war elephants remains one of the most audacious feats in military history. Despite losing most of his elephants and thousands of his men in the Alpine snows he managed to bring the bulk of his army safely into the newly created Roman province of Cisalpine Gaul, near the modern city of Turin.

He had also managed to outflank the enemy force sent to block his path along the coast, and his army now stood on Roman soil. Publius Cornelius Scipio's Roman army was

Below: A reconstruction of the naval harbor of Carthage, Tunisia, as it would have looked during Hannibal's time.

recalled by sea, and marched to meet Hannibal's army near Placentia. At the Battle of the Trebbia that followed, the Romans were defeated, and the road south lay open to the Carthaginians. Hannibal spent the winter in the Po valley, recruiting Gallic tribesmen to his standard, but in the spring of 217 BC he resumed his march. An army commanded by Consul Gaius Flaminius tried to block his path near Lake Trasimene, but the Roman commander was outmaneuvered and ambushed, and his army was destroyed by the wily Hannibal. The road to Rome now lay open.

Hannibal realized that he lacked the siege equipment needed to capture Rome, so instead he tried to starve the city into submission by conquering its Italian hinterland. However, Hannibal met his match in the new Roman consul Fabius Maximus, whose "fabian" tactics of avoiding battle while limiting his enemy's options proved their worth. However, this lack of aggression proved unpopular in Rome, and in 216 BC the consuls raised a new powerful army, and offered battle. Hannibal accepted the challenge, and the two sides met in the plains of Apulia. The Battle of Cannae that followed was a

Left: Hannibal during his campaign in Italy, from a 16th century fresco by Jacopo Ripanda.
Below: Cannae, near modern Barletta, Italy, where in 216 BC Hannibal inflicted on the Roman army the severest defeat ever sustained by Rome.

resounding victory for Hannibal, whose army enveloped the larger Roman army, then slaughtered it. It was the greatest defeat ever suffered by the Romans throughout their long history.

The rest of the war proved an anticlimax for Hannibal. Rome remained unconquered, and for the most part its armies reverted to their successful "fabian" tactics. Instead it sent troops overseas to pacify Spain and Sicily. The stalemate in Italy continued for a decade, until finally, in 203 BC, Hannibal was recalled to Carthage to defend the city from a Roman army commanded by Scipio "Africanus." In 202 BC the two commanders met at the Battle of Zama, and this time it was the Romans who emerged victorious. When Carthage sued for peace in 200 BC Hannibal briefly became a politician, but in 195 BC he went into self-imposed exile, determined to continue the fight against his sworn enemies.

For more than a decade Hannibal remained a political thorn in Rome's side, encouraging rulers such as Antiochus III of Seleucia and King Prusias of Bythnia to make a stand against Roman expansion. Hannibal eventually died in exile in 183 BC, at the age of sixty-four. For almost half a century he had been Rome's greatest foe, but for all his military genius he found himself unable to strike the killing blow, and it was Rome rather than Carthage that ultimately emerged as the victor.

Below: The War Elephants of Alexander the Great, from a 15th century French manuscript portraying the life of the Macedonian king. In fact it was Hannibal rather than Alexander who used elephants in combat.

Hasdrubal Barca
(d. 207 BC)
Carthaginian General

The younger brother of Hannibal, Hasdrubal fought in Italy against the Scipio brothers, defeated king Syphax and his Numedian army in Africa, and destroyed the Roman army at the Battle of the Upper Baetis. Hasdrubal was eventually defeated by the Romans and killed at the Battle of Metaurus in 207 BC.

Left: The defense of Carthage, in which Hasdrubal Barca, brother of Hannibal, took part.

Hanno the Elder
(d. 204 BC)
Carthaginian General

Hanno aided Hannibal in his victory over the Gauls in 218 BC but was defeated by the Roman army near Gumentum. In 215 BC Hanno aided Hannibal at the Battle of Nola, but was intercepted by Gaius Grachhus and defeated at Beneventum the following year. In 212 BC Hanno was again defeated while trying to relieve Capua from the Roman siege.

Hasdrubal "the Fair"
(c.221 BC)
Carthaginian General

Hasdrubal served under his father-in-law Hamilcar Barca in his campaign against the rulers of Carthage at the end of the First Punic Wars. Using skilful diplomacy he extended the empire after the death of Hamilcar and established the new capital of Carthago Nova. Hasdrubal's treaty with the Roman Republic established boundaries between the two powers.

Hector
Trojan War (mythological)
Trojan Prince

Leader in the defense of Troy, Hector challenged Ajax to single combat. The day-long fight did not produce a winner but inspired mutual expressions of admiration. When Achilles routed the Trojans back to their city, only Hector stood to face him. Achilles killed Hector, but not before Hector promised that Paris would avenge his death.

Horemheb
(1320-1292 BC)
Egyptian Pharaoh

Heir to Tutankhamun's throne, Horemheb introduced several reforms. He decentralized power by appointing numerous regional judges, and diminished the influence of the priesthood by selecting priests from loyalists within the army. Horemheb built numerous temples throughout Egypt and restored much of the power and influence of Egypt during his twenty-eight-year reign.

Below: A granite statue of the Pharaoh Horemheb, discovered in Luxor, Egypt, in 1989. The pharaoh is depicted making offerings to the Egyptian god Atum.

Joshua
(c.1200 BC)
Hebrew Leader

According to the Bible, Joshua was born in Egypt during the Israelite enslavement. He accompanied Moses on the Exodus and defeated the Amalekites in Rephidim. Joshua conquered the land of Canaan, culminating in the Battle of Gibeon, and divided the land among the tribes of Israel. Joshua died at the age of 110.

Above: Joshua at the battle fought before the walls of Jericho, depicted in a French lithograph of the late 18th century.

Judas Maccabeus
(c.167-160 BC)
Jewish General

Jugurtha
(c.154-104 BC, ruled 118-104 BC)
King of Numidia

Judas led the Maccabean revolt against the Seleucid Empire. He drove his enemies out of Judea and restored the Temple of Jerusalem in 164 BC, now celebrated as the Jewish holiday of Hanukkah. Judas was killed in the Battle of Elasa (16 0BC) but resistance continued for several years after his death until independence was finally won.

The ruler of a semi-nomadic North African people, Jugurtha angered Rome and prompted a war that lasted for seven years. Despite Jugurtha's initial success he was eventually defeated by Gaius Marius, and his Numidian resistance collapsed following his capture and execution.

Above: Judas Macabbeaus, from a 19th century color engraving of the Old Testament.

Above: Jugartha, King of Numidia, once a friend and then an enemy of Rome, from a silver coin of the 2nd century BC.

Julian (Flavius Claudius Julianus)
(332-363 AD)
Roman Emperor

Julian was born in Constantinople, the son of Julius Constantius, half brother of Constantine the Great. Julian had a strict Christian upbringing for several years, but this was contrasted with a Greek education when he moved to Athens.

In 355 AD Julian set out to stabilize the Rhine frontier, which was under pressure from Alamanni attacks, but was defeated near Rheims. Julian repelled a surprise Alamanni attack in 357 AD and then took over command of all Roman forces in Gaul. He destroyed a force of 30,000 Alamanni

Above: Emperor Julian "the Apostate," portrayed on a Roman silver solidus of the mid-4th century AD.
Right: A marble statue of Emperor Julian, wearing a Greek academic cloak, and a crown representing Roman divinity.

near Argentoratum and raided across the Rhine. Julian became emperor following the death of Constantius in 361 AD. He proposed an invasion of Persia and departed from Antioch in 363 AD at the head of his 65,000-strong army. His force was held by the defenses of Ctesiphon and, suffering from a lack of supplies and repeated Persian attacks, he ordered a retreat. Julian was killed in one of these minor engagements.

Although he was an energetic and skilful general, Julian's Persian campaign was ill-judged and his toleration of the Pagan religion failed to revive these traditional beliefs in the face of Christian hostility.

Julius Caesar
(c100-44 BC)
Republican Roman Statesman and General

Gaius Julius Caesar was born into one of the oldest patrician families in Rome, but his childhood was marred by political turmoil created in part by Caesar's uncle, the general Gaius Marius. Although Marius died in 86 BC his supporters continued to rule in his name, until the general's former protégé, Sulla, crushed the Marian faction in 82 BC. As a relative of Marius Caesar's name appeared on Sulla's death lists, so he and his family fled Rome until Sulla agreed to spare his life. Rather than return home, the young Caesar joined the army, and served with distinction in Asia, earning recognition for his heroism during the siege of Mytilene. After the death of Sulla in 78 BC Caesar returned to Rome, and soon established a reputation as an orator. He subsequently held various political and religious offices before becoming provincial governor in 62 BC. His subsequent campaigns in Spain proved extremely successful, and he returned to Rome in triumph.

His great political breakthrough came in 59 BC when he formed a three-sided alliance with the veteran general Pompey and the magnate Crassus, Between them they controlled the Senate, and so Caesar was duly elected consul. This Triumvirate proved highly successful, and when his term in office was over

Caesar arranged another governorship, this time in Cisalpine Gaul. Transalpine Gaul was added later, giving Caesar control of a powerful army. Rome's Gallic allies soon faced the threat of invasion by the Germanic Helvetii, and Caesar seized the opportunity this provided. After defeating the Helvetii and their allies the Suebi in 58 BC his army remained in Gaul for the winter. Caesar recruited more troops, and the follow-

Above: A marble bust of Julius Caesar, who recorded his own military exploits, providing us with a fascinating if slightly colored account of his campaigns.

ing spring he launched a full-scale conquest of the Gallic heartland.

In 57 BC he moved north into the land of the Belgae. He defeated the various Belgic tribes before they could unite, and he even managed to detach a legion to conquer Armorica

Above: The assassination of Julius Caesar by Brutus and his fellow conspirators.

(now Brittany). In 56 BC his proconsulship was renewed for another five years, which secured his political position back in Rome. He returned to the fray, and by the winter of 56 BC only the northernmost Gallic tribes remained unconquered. The following year he repelled a Germanic incursion over the River Rhine, and led a brief reconnaissance to Britain. He returned there the following year, advancing as far as the River Thames before news of a revolt in Gaul forced him to return to the continental mainland. After defeating the rebel Ambiorix he considered Gaul to be fully pacified, but an even larger revolt erupted in 52 BC, led by Vercingetorix. After several battles and sieges Caesar eventually cornered the Gallic leader at Alesia, and after a lengthy siege he forced Vercingetorix to surrender. Gaul was now completely subdued.

However, all was not well in Rome. The Triumvirate had collapsed, and in 50 AD Pompey ordered Caesar to disband his army. Caesar responded by crossing the Rubicon stream that marked the frontier and marching on Rome itself. This act meant civil war. Pompey and the senate fled to Greece, leaving Rome and Italy to Caesar. The following year Caesar marched in pursuit, and in 48 BC the armies of Pompey

Above: Julius Caesar receiving the surrender of Vercingetorix, the Gallic leader who was cornered and besieged by Caesar at Alesia in 52 BC (from a painting by Henri Paul Motte).

and Caesar clashed at Dyrrhachium on the Adriatic coast. Pompey was defeated, and withdrew inland to Pharsalus, where the two armies met again. Once again Caesar won the battle, forcing Pompey to flee to Egypt. Caesar pursued him, only to discover that his rival had been murdered. Caesar lingered in Egypt for a year, siding with his lover Queen Cleopatra in a civil war against her brother, King Ptolemy XIII. Caesar

Following page: A modern depiction by Henri Paul Motte of the siege of Alesia. Caesar ringed Alesia with a double line of fortifications—to contain the defenders and to repel any relief force.

and Cleopatra defeated Ptolemy in 47 BC, and Cleopatra was installed on the throne.

In 46 BC Caesar resumed the war against Pompey's allies and supporters, defeating them in Asia Minor, North Africa, and finally in Spain, where the civil war officially ended following Caesar's victory at Munda. He returned to Rome in triumph in 45 BC, and the following year a cowed Senate proclaimed him "Dictator for Life." However, his enemies were circling, and on the Ides of March of 44 BC they struck. Caesar was assassinated in the Senate by a group of sixry senators who included Cassius, Casca, and Brutus, the son of Caesar's mistress. The assassins thought they had disposed of an unpopular tyrant, but Caesar's ally, Mark Antony, roused the Romans against the assassins, who were forced to flee the city. This second phase of civil war continued for another fourteen years, until Caesar's adopted son Octavian emerged victorious. Octavian had himself proclaimed emperor, adopting the name Caesar Augustus in honor of his adoptive father. Caesar remains one of the great military commanders of history, his achievements surpassing all but those of Alexander the Great.

Left: This bronze statue of Julius Caesar, cast during the 1st century AD, now stands in the northern Italian town of Aosta.
Right: A modern reconstruction of the Roman defenses built by Julius Caesar's army to encircle the Gallic-held stronghold of Alesia in 52 BC.

Gaius Marius

(157-86 BC)
Republican Roman Statesman and General

One of Rome's great unsung military heroes, Gaius Marius was the man responsible for transforming the Roman army into a professional force, a military machine capable of sweeping all before it. However, this achievement and his numerous military successes were set against the political damage he caused during his final years. Unlike most future Roman Consuls, Marius was born in Arpinum (now Arpino) rather than in Rome itself, and thus he was considered a political outsider.

He joined the army as a young officer, and in 134 BC his exploits in Numidia earned him the praise of Scipio Africanus. After several attempts at gaining elected office he was finally returned as a tribune of the plebians in 120 BC—the first rung on the Senatorial ladder. However, his populist line antagonized many conservatives. Four years later he was named as the new governor of Lusitania (now Portugal), another step up the political ladder.

On his return to Rome he married into the patrician Julii family, which gave him greater status within Rome and made him a more acceptable consular candidate. However, he was still considered a "new man". Therefore in 109 BC he returned to active service. As a Roman legate he served as the army's deputy commander during the successful Jugarthine War in North Africa, and two years later Marius drew on this display of military ability when he stood in the Consular elections.

Marius won, and his first act as consul was to take over command of

the army in Africa. Rome was short of troops, so Marius decided to waive the normal selection procedures based on social class, and replace it with a professional military structure, where selection for the army was open to all Romans, regardless of means. The

Left: A marble bust of the veteran Roman general Gaius Marius, who reformed the Roman army and served seven terms as consul.
Above: Disembarkation of Caesar's troops.

result was to transform the Roman army from a largely amateur citizen army into a professional fighting force—the basis of the Roman legion that would dominate the ancient world for another four centuries. The organization of the legion was also changed, becoming easier to control in battle, and better suited to the style of fighting the Romans favored. By opening up recruitment to Romans of all social strata Marius greatly increased the potential pool of volunteers, allowing the army to expand dramatically during the years that followed.

Above: Reconstruction of a Roman officer's helmet of the mid to late 1st century AD.

Marius remained with the army. After a detour north of the Alps the Cimrii began to move south again in 102 BC, but Marius left a blocking force to face them while he marched his main army north to deal with another tribe, the Teutones, who were moving through southern Gaul. He defeated the Teutones at the Battle of Aqae Sextae, but his rearguard was unable to prevent the Cimri from reaching the plains of Northern Italy. In 101 BC he caught up with the Cimrii near Vercellae and inflicted a crushing defeat on them. Rome was spared, and as a reward Marius was elected as consul for a sixth time.

Marius retired at the end of his consulship, but in 91 BC Rome faced a new threat—a revolt by its Italian allies—and Marius resumed control of the army, with the patrician Sulla as his deputy. The two men eventually fell out, and factional fighting soon developed into a civil war. Sulla's troops seized Rome, and Marius fled to Africa. Then in 87 BC, when Sulla was campaigning in Greece, Marius returned and recaptured the city. Sulla was officially exiled, and as Marius was elected consul for a seventh time his supporters sought bloody revenge against the pro-Sullan faction. However, the seventy-one-year-old Marius died suddenly, leaving a power vacuum that was soon filled by a vengeful Sulla, who returned to reclaim his capital. This vendetta all but destroyed the Roman Republic, and cast a shadow over the otherwise exceptional career of one of Rome's finest military commanders.

During 107 BC Marius tested his new legions in battle against King Jugartha of Numidia, and he secured a victory within two years, aided in part by the clandestine actions of his lieutenant Lucius Cornelius Sulla, who managed to capture Jugartha. However, Marius was about to face a bigger challenge.

In 109 BC the Germanic Cimrii people invaded southern Gaul, and over the next four years later they defeated two more Roman armies sent to check their migration towards the Roman frontier. In 105 BC Marius was elected consul again, and ordered to save Rome. In fact the campaign lasted for four years, and the consulship was renewed each time while

Leonidas
(reigned 489-480 BC)
King of Sparta

Leonidas, (meaning "Lion-like" or "Lion's Son") was the son of King Anaxandridas II of Sparta, and according to Spartan legend was a descendant of Heracles, son of Zeus. When his father died he was succeeded by Leonidas' half-brother Cleomines, who used his highly trained and motivated Spartan army to enlarge the boundaries of the Spartan city state, and to increase its political standing within the Aegean.

Above: Léonidas aux Thermopyles—King Leonidas of Sparta, in a painting by Jacques Louis David, 1814.

Leonidas married Cleomines' daughter Gorgo, and succeeded him following the king's death in or around 489 BC. He was a staunch opponent of King Xerxes of Persia, and in 480 BC

bodyguard formed the core of the Greek force of around 4,200 men that subsequently gathered at the Pass of Thermopylae to bar Xerxes' path. Although Leonidas was greatly outnumbered, the narrow pass between the mountains and the sea served as a funnel, which made numbers far less important than troop quality. For two days Leonidas and his men repulsed every frontal attack the Persians launched at them, and Persian casualties were estimated at around 20,000 men, for the loss of only a handful of Spartans. Reputedly, two of Xerxes' brothers died while leading the assaults.

However, Xerxes kept his elite "Immortals" in reserve, and on the third day a local shepherd in Persian pay guided their commander Hydarnes along a mountain path that brought him out behind the Spartan position. Realizing that further resistance was futile, Leonidas ordered part of his army to retreat to safety, while he and his 300 Spartans (supported by another 1,900 Greek troops) made a last stand, in order to cover the retreat. The small Greek force was set upon from all sides, and died to a man. According to the Greek historian Herodotus, Xerxes had the body of Leonidas crucified. However, Leonidas' heroic resistance emboldened the Greeks, and the following year the Persians would be driven from Greek soil.

he rejected Persian attempts to secure his loyalty, and instead sided with the alliance of Greek city states that had banded together to oppose the Persian king.

When Xerxes invaded Greece in the spring of 480 BC Leonidas led his Spartan army north to join the fight. Although most of his men served with the Greek fleet, his 300-man

廉頗

羸戟不克何謀不忠文疑季疑將
相和裏保衛社稷氣爭公功大臣之
彦名將之風 醉墨黄亭于 盥書

Marcus Aemilius Lepidus
(d. 13 BC)
Republican Roman General and Statesman

Lepidus was a former loyal deputy of Julius Caesar, and after the dictator's death in 44 BC, he became a member of the "Second Triumvirate" alongside Octavian and Mark Antony, and together they crushed Caesar's assassins. Lepidus was later accused of attempting to seize power from Octavian, and was stripped of his power and exiled to his estates.

Lian Po
(c. 450-220 BC)
Chinese Zhao General

Lian Po was a leading general from the state of Zhao, one of the "Warring States" of north and central China whose conflicts dominated the region for almost three centuries. He reorganized the army of Zhao after its defeat at the Battle of Changping (260 BC), and was widely regarded as the leading military figure of the period.

Left: Llan Po, whose military methods were studied for centuries after his death.

Licinius
(c.250-325 AD, reigned 308-324 AD)
Roman Emperor

In 308 AD the experienced Roman general Flavius Galerius Licinius became the Western Roman Emperor, although by 314 AD a civil war erupted between him and his Eastern counterpart, Constantine "the Great." Licinius was defeated at the Battle of Adrianople (324 AD), and was killed by his rival the following year.

Above: The Western Roman Emperor Licinius, as depicted in a commemorative salver dating from the early 4th century AD.

Liu Bei

(161-223 AD)
Chinese Warlord and Shu Han Emperor

An important Chinese warlord and one of the founders of the Three Kingdoms, Liu Bei came from humble origins, but proved a highly successful leader. Although he relied on his military commander Zhuge Liang to win his victories, it was Liu Bei's strategic vision that helped forge his state into an empire.

Left: While escaping from a superior force led by his rival Cao Cao, the Chinese warlord Liu Be delayed his flight in order to transport refugees across the Han River.

Lu Bu

(150-199 AD)
Chinese Han Warlord

Regarded as one of the most successful military commanders of the Three Kingdoms era, despite his reputation for duplicity, Lu Bu was later seen as a romantic hero, celebrated in Chinese medieval literature. He was eventually captured and killed by Cao Cao, a rival warlord.

Left: During a parley with the rival warlords Lieu Bei and Yuan Shu, Lu Shu showed his skill as an archer, in an attempt to demonstrate the futility of continued fighting.

Lysimachus
(355-281 BC)
Macedonian General

Above: A marble bust of Lyisimachus, the Macedonian general who became the ruler of Thrace.

Born in Macedon in 355, Lysimachus served with distinction in Alexander's bodyguard in Persia. He played little part in the succession wars after Alexander's death, but was involved in the alliance against Antigonus and his son Demetrius, and played a significant part in their defeat at Ipsus in 301 BC. For this Lysimachus was awarded extensive territory in Asia.

Lysimachus fought further battles against Demetrius, capturing Greek cities on the Ionian coast (301-294 BC). This was followed by an unsuccessful campaign beyond the Danube, which led to a brief period of imprisonment. Hostilities against Demetrius recommenced when Lysimachus joined forces with Pyrrhus of Epirus and invaded Macedon (288-286 BC), driving Demetrius from the throne.

The fortunes of Lysimachus deteriorated dramatically when Arsinoë, his third wife, persuaded him to execute his own son Agathocles on dubious charges of treason with King Seleucus (thus allowing her own children to succeed to the throne). This act caused widespread disgust throughout the realm, and the resulting disorder gave Seleucus the opportunity to invade. When Lysimachus met the invading force at Corupedium in Asia Minor (281 BC) he was defeated and killed.

Lysimachus was an able and energetic ruler, a competent but not exceptional commander, whose legacy was tragically ruined by suspicion of his son's loyalty.

Magnus Maximus
(c.335-388 AD)
Roman General and Imperial Usurper

In 383 AD the Roman army in Britain proclaimed the General Maximus Maximus as their emperor, and after leading his men over to Gaul he defeated and killed the Emperor Gratian. The usurper was in turn defeated and captured by Theodosius and the child Emperor Valentian II at the Battle of the Save (388 AD), and was executed shortly afterwards.

Mark Antony (Marcus Antonius)
(83-30 BC)
Republican Roman General

Born in Rome in 83BC, Mark Antony was a distant cousin of Caesar. Said to be a reckless in youth, he fled to Greece to escape gambling debts. In 54 BC, Antony served in Caesar's staff during the Gallic Wars and he supported Caesar when he led his

Right: A marble bust of the Roman general Mark Antony, supporter of Julius Caesar but foe of Caesar's adopted son Octavian.
Below: The dying Mark Antony is presented to his lover, Queen Cleopatra, in a mid-19th century painting by Ernest Hillemacher.

army across the Rubicon into Italy.

Born in Rome in 83 BC, Mark Antony was a distant cousin of Caesar. Said to be reckless in youth, he fled to Greece to escape gambling debts. In 54 BC Antony served in Caesar's staff during the Gallic Wars, and he supported Caesar when the famous general led his army across the Rubicon into Italy.

Following Caesar's assassination, Antony publicly shamed his murderers at Caesar's funeral, which led to public attacks on the assassins. Antony and his ally Octavian defeated the conspiritors Brutus and Cassius at Philippi in 42 BC. Antony then traveled to Egypt where he allied himself with Queen Cleopatra VII, the former lover of Julius Caesar, who lent him money to raise another army. Antony invaded the Parthian Empire but the campaign was a disaster and Antony lost most of his army during its retreat.

Antony was summoned to Rome, but remained in Alexandria with Cleopatra. In 32 BC, the Senate declared war against Cleopatra. Octavian, Antony's former ally, sent a fleet that destroyed the navy of Antony and Cleopatra navy at the Battle of Actium in 31 BC, and then invaded Egypt the following year. With nowhere left to hide, Antony committed suicide. Following his death Octavian became the uncontested ruler of Rome.

Memnon of Rhodes
(380-333 BC)
Greek Mercenary General

The well-respected commander of the Greek mercenary contingent in the Persian army of Darius III, Memnon advised his paymaster to avoid battle with Alexander the Great, and to conduct a "scorched earth" policy. He was ignored, and Alexander proved victorious. A year later Memnon died defending the Ionian city of Mytelene against Alexander's army.

Merneptah
(reigned 1213-1203 BC)
Egyptian Pharaoh

Merneptah was the thirteenth son of Ramesses II. He came to power in his sixties after his older brothers had died. Merneptah successfully campaigned against the Libyans and the tribes of Israel. He moved Egypt's capital from Piramesse back to Memphis, and was succeeded by his son Seti II.

Above: A granite bust of the Pharaoh Merneptah, the successor of Ramses II.

Miltiades (the Younger)
(550–489 BC)
Athenian General

Miltiades was a vassal of Darius I of Persia, joining his campaign against the Scythians in 513 BC. Later, he switched sides, joining the Ionian revolt of 499 BC against Persian rule, and went on to establish friendly relations with Athens. He fled there in 492 BC when the revolt collapsed.

When he returned to Athens, Miltiades was not well received because of his service with the Persians. However, he was able to convince the people there that he still had Greek interests at heart, and managed to avoid punishment. Miltiades was made a general and is thought to have formulated tactics that led to the defeat of the Persians at the Battle of Marathon in 490 BC. In 489 BC Miltiades led a fleet of seventy ships against Páros and other Greek islands considered loyal to the Persians. Miltiades failed to take the island and was badly wounded during the campaign.

On his return to Athens, Miltiades's failure attracted charges of treason and he was sentenced to death. This was later reduced to a fine of fifty talents. This sum was impossibly high and Miltiades was sent to prison where he died, possibly because of an infection in his wound.

Right: A Greek marble bust of Miltiades "the Younger," dating from the early 4th century BC.

Mithridates VI "Eupator"
(132-63 BC)
King of Pontus

The young Mithridates succeeded his father when he was twelve, but during his minority the kingdom was ruled by his mother Gespaepyris. When he was seventeen he had his mother imprisoned, and so secured control of the throne. To safeguard his position he also killed several of his brothers. He planned to make his small kingdom on the northern shore of Asia Minor into a major regional power, so he devoted his resources to building up the Pontic army. First he campaigned in Colchis (now Georgia), then secured suzerainty over the Scythians, who lay further to the north. In Asia Minor Mithridates invaded Bithynia, then a Roman ally, which made a war with Rome inevitable.

In the First Mithraditic War (90-85 BC) that followed he overran the coastal cities of western Asia Minor, and massacred more than 80,000 Roman citizens there. When many Greek cities declared their support for him he crossed the Aegean, where he was met by a Roman army commanded by Sulla. The Roman general captured Athens, and then defeated Mithridates at the Battle of Chaeronea (86 BC). The Pontic army retreated back to Asia Minor, and Sulla reconquered the lost cities. A temporary peace was signed in 85 BC, but conflict broke out again as soon as

Sulla returned to Rome. Mithridates had been defeated but not vanquished. When the Romans tried to annex Bythnia Mithradates attacked them, forcing the Romans to withdraw.

A fragile peace lasted until 75 BC, when Lucullus invaded Pontus, driving Mithridates from his cities into the Pontic mountains. The Pontic army proved no match for Lucullus' veteran Roman legionaries. However, the war lingered on until 69 BC, so the Senate sent Pompey to replace Lucullus, with orders to deal with the Pontic king once and for all. By 63 BC

he had been driven out of Asia Minor, and took refuge in his stronghold of Panticapaeum (now Kerch, in the Crimea). He hoped his sons would support him, but when they refused Mithridates was left with no more allies. He duly committed suicide, and on his death Pontus officially became a Roman satellite.

Above: A silver tetradrachme coin of the reign of Mithradites VI, bearing the images of grazing deer, and a star and crescent.
Right: The reverse of the same Pontic coin features a portrait of King Mithridates VI of Pontus.

Nebuchadnezzar II (the Great)

(c.605-561 BC)
King of Babylonia

Nebuchadnezzar fought to increase Babylonian influence in Syria and Judah. He captured Jerusalem, destroyed the temple, and deported many of its inhabitants to Babylon. Following this Nebuchadnezzar conducted a thirteen-year siege of Tyr, after which the Tyrians accepted Babylonian authority. Nebuchadnezzar completed many building projects, including the Hanging Gardens of Babylon,

Top: It is said that Hebrews were tossed into a furnace for refusing to worship Nebuchadnezzar's gold statue (from a 6h century fresco).
Above: Nebuchezzar II, King of Babylon, on his throne, in a bronze decorative detail from a set of Italian medieval doors.

Septimius Odaenathus (or Odenatus, Odainath)

(d. 267 AD)
Palmyrene Governor and Roman General

Odaenathus was born in Palmyra. A Romanized Arab, he became chief of the Palmyrenes in 251 AD. He achieved Roman consular rank in 258 AD and was married to the famous Zenobia of Syria.

As a Roman ally he attacked the Persian army, which was laden with plunder following the sack of Antioch in 261 AD, defeating them before they

Above: The ruins of the Cardo Maximus, or "Great Collonade," an example of 2nd century AD Roman town planning in Palmyra, Syria.

could cross the Euphrates. Odaenathus allied himself to Gallienus, the son and successor to Valerian, and defeated the usurper Quietus at Emesa in 262 AD. Later that year He was rewarded with the position of viceroy of all the East. In a series of campaigns he went on to defeat Shapur in Persia and forced him to sue for peace in 264 AD. This restored Roman rule in the East, and the Emperor Gallienus awarded Odaenathus a triumph, where his captives and trophies were displayed. In 267 AD, on his way to fight the Goths in Cappadocia, Odaenathus was murdered by his nephew Maeonius.

An immensely capable general, Odaenathus remained loyal to his Roman overlords but was in essence a Palmyrene patriot whose aim was to create an independent empire in the Levant. He was succeeded by his wife Zenobia, who governed Palmyra on behalf of her son Vaballathus.

Odysseus
Trojan War
Greek Hero (mythological)

Legendary Greek king of Ithaca, hero of Homer's epic, the *Odyssey*, renowned for his cunning, Odysseus devised the Trojan Horse. He experienced many adventures in his ten-year journey back from the wars, and returned home to find his wife beset by suitors. Odysseus killed the suitors and restored his kingdom.

Above: Odysseus returning form the Trojan War, tied to the mast of his ship to avoid temptation by the Sirens.
Following page: Ulysses on the Island of the Phacacians during his epic voyage (from a painting Peter Paul Rubens).

Orodes II (also called Hyrodes
(reigned 57-38 BC)
King of Parthia

The son of the Great King Pheaates III, Orodes was no admirer of his father, who had allied himself with the Romans rather than Parthia's natural ally, King Mithradates of Pontus. As a result Orodes found himself a hostage of Pompey "the Great," and the Romans betrayed Pheaates' trust by occupying his western provinces. Consequently, in 57 BC, Orodes and his brother Prince Mithradates murdered their father, and claimed the Parthian throne for themselves. Mithradates was given Media to rule, but his heavy-handed control led to a revolt, and he was deposed. Orodes crushed the revolt and claimed Media for himself. Mithradites invaded Parthia with a rebel army, but he was defeated, and then eventually captured at Babylon, where he was killed on the orders of his brother.

Meanwhile, Marcus Crassus had become governor of Roman Syria, and in 54 BC he crossed the Euphrates River and invaded Parthia. His expedition had been poorly planned, and his infantry lacked the cavalry support and supplies they needed to campaign effectively in the Parthian desert. Orodes sent his foot archers to contain Crassus' Armenian allies, while he led the rest of his army—all cavalry—to intercept the Roman column. His horse archers kept their distance, harassing the Roman legionaries, who were unable to shoot back. Eventually Crassus' force was surrounded, and its survivors were forced to surrender. Crassus was known for his greed, so when Orodes met the Roman commander he ordered molten gold to be poured down his throat.

Orodes followed this crushing victory by invading Armenia, and forcing their ruler to renege on his treaty with the Romans. The Parthian king bided his time during the Roman Civil Wars, but in 40 BC he ordered his son Prince Pacorus to invade Syria, and he successfully conquered most of the province. Pacorus was killed during a campaign against the Romans in Asia Minor two years later, and so Orodes appointed his younger son Phraates as his heir. He was rewarded shortly afterwards when the Parthian king was murdered by his son, who duly claimed the throne for himself.

Above: Head and shoulders of a bronze statue of a Parthian warrior (now displayed in the Archaeological Museum, Teheran). Orodes was the self-proclaimed king of Parthia during 57-58 BC.

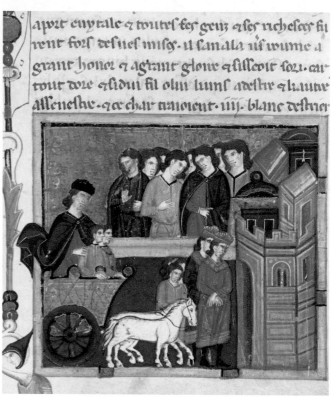

Otho
(32-69 AD)
Roman Emperor

Lucius Aemilius Paullus "Macedonicus"
(229 BC-160 BC)
Republican Roman General

Marcus Salvius Otho was one of the contenders for the Imperial crown during "The Year of the Four Emperors" (69 AD). He killed his rival Galba in a palace coup, but was defeated by Vitellius later that year, and was forced to take his own life.

Above: The Roman Emperor Otho, another of the contenders of 69 AD —"The Year of the Four Emperors," from a late 16th century engraving.

Paullus fought in Hispania against the Lusitanians in 191 BC, won the Battle of Pydna in 168 BC, sacked the towns of Epirus whom he suspected of having Macedonian sympathies, and enslaved its population even though the kingdom had already been pacified. Paullus was awarded a triumph on his return to Rome for the immense riches he delivered.

Above: A triumphant Paullus having defeated the Macedonians ad ended the Third Macedonian War in 168 BC.

Pausanias
(c.479 BC)
Spartan General

Perdiccas
(d. 320 BC)
Macedonian General

Spartan regent who captured Byzantium but released prisoners allied to the Persian king, His loyalty questioned, he was recalled to Sparta. Letters to Xerses were discovered and suspicions were confirmed. Pausanias escaped arrest and hid in a temple, but it was walled up and ringed with sentries to starve him out, He died shortly after being brought out.

On the death of Alexander the Great, Perdiccas was made regent and protector of Alexander's heir. He proved unable to prevent the partition of Alexander's territories between the "Successor Generals,"and was assassinated in Egypt while campaigning against the "Successor" Ptolemy.

Above: Greek hoplites in battle, a detail from a Greek vase produced during the early 5th century BC.

Philip II
(383–336 BC)
King of Macedon

Philip was born in Pella, the youngest son of King Amyntas III. Held hostage as a youth in Thebes, Philip learned the art of war under General Epaminondas. On his return to Macedon he became regent for his nephew Amyntas. As a regent, between 359 and 356BC Philip fought many wars to preserve the kingdom, against the Paeonians, the Illyrians, and the Athenians. In 356 BC he was crowned king following the death of his elder brothers.

Captured gold and silver mines at Crenides provided the revenue that allowed Philip to greatly strengthen his army. In the following year he lost an eye in battle but went on to conquer Thessaly in 352 BC. Philip made peace with Athens in 346 BC but continued diplomatic maneuverings to tighten Macedonian control over Greece. In 340 BC he attacked Byzantium and destroyed an Athenian-Theban army at Chaeronea in 338 BC, giving Philip control of much of Greece apart from Sparta. Philip was murdered at the wedding of his daughter Cleopatra in 336 BC.

Philip had a great appreciation for Greek culture and developed Macedonia into a worthy Grecian

Right: Philip II, King of Macedon, as depicted in a 14th century Byzantine manuscript recounting the life of his son Alexander "the Great."

state. He was also a skilled and courageous general, wily diplomat, and superb military organizer. The army that his son, Alexander the Great, inherited was truly of Philip's making.

Above: Ruins of the *Philippeion*, a circular temple built at Olympia in Greece by Philip II to celebrate his victory at the Battle of Chaeronea. It was completed by his son Alexander.

Right: A Macedonian gold stater coin, bearing a depiction of King Philip II.

115

Philip V
(238-179 BC, reigned 221-179 BC)
King of Macedon

In 229 BC the nine-year-old Philip succeeded his father Demetrius II as King of Macedon, although real power rested in the hands of his cousin, Antigonus Dosun, who remained regent for just two years. Then, in 227 BC, Antigonus married the late king's widow, and proclaimed himself King Antigonus III. At that time the Greek city states were divided into two power blocks—the Achaean League led by Aratus of Sycion, and the Aeolian League led by King Cleomenes III of Sparta. Antigonus allied himself with the Achaeans, and in 222 BC he defeated Cleomenes at the Battle of Sellasia. However, the self-appointed king died the following year, and Philip, by then seventeen years of age, duly succeeded him in late 221 BC.

King Philip's first challenge was to finish his predecessor's war campaign against the Illyrians and the neighboring Dardani tribe, who had invaded Macedonia. Then he turned his attention to Greece, where a new Aetolian coalition was forming. Philip countered this by forming a new, pro-Macedonian coalition known as the Hellenic League, and the war that followed eventually ended in a Hellenic victory. Philip turned his attention to Rome.

In 216 BC Philip invaded Roman Illyria, but the operation was abandoned following the loss of the Macedonian fleet. The Romans were too busy fighting the Carthaginians to spare troops, so instead they formed an alliance with the Spartans and their Aetolian allies, forcing Philip to campaign in southern Greece. The war soon reached a stalemate, and a temporary peace was concluded in 206 BC.

Five years later the Romans finally conquered Carthage, and so were able to deal with Philip. War was declared in 200 BC, and three years later Philip's Macedonian army was decisively defeated by the Romans at the Battle of Cynoscephalae. The war ended when Philip signed a humiliating peace treaty and paid the Romans a fortune in reparations. He was also forced to cooperate with the Romans when they turned on the Spartans (195

Above: The marble funerary stele of a hoplite from the site of the royal burial ground at Verghina in Macedonia, dating from the 3rd century BC.

BC), and the Seleucids (192-189 BC). On Philip's death, Macedonia had become little more than a Roman puppet state.

Phyrrus of Epirus
(318-272 BC)
King of Epirus

Below: King Phyrrus of Epirus, as depicted in a 3rd century BC Roman bust.
Bottom: King Phyrrus killing Polyxena at the tomb of her father, King Priam of Troy, in a painting by Vincenzo Ferreri, 1793.

Piye
(reigned 752-721 BC)
Egyptian Pharaoh

Second cousin to Alexander, and prince of a successor state, a successful general and one of Rome's toughest opponents, Phyrrus enjoyed victories, but they usually came at high price (hence a "Pyrrhic victory"). He defeated the Romans at Heraclea in 280 BC and Asculum in 279 BC, fought the Carthaginians, and invaded Macedonia. He died during confused street-fighting in Argos.

Founder of the 25th Dynasty of Egypt, Piye formed a coalition of local kings, invaded Middle and Lower Eqypt, conquered Hermopolis and Memphis, and accepted the surrender of the kings of the Nile Delta. Piye conquered Egypt and ruled from Napata, a city in Nubia, His reign lasted for about thirty years.

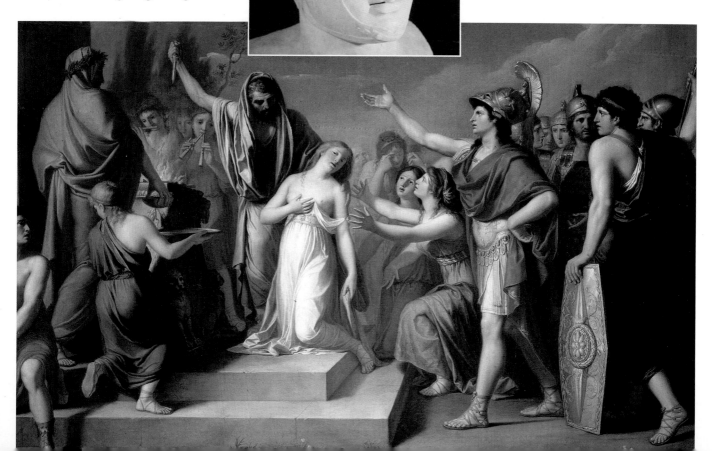

Gnaeus Pompey "the Great"
(106-48 BC)
Republican Roman General and Statesman

One of Rome's great unsung military heroes, Gnaeus Pompey was born into a wealthy rural family, and he inherited the family estates in 87 BC. During the political struggle between Marius and Sulla the young Pompey sided with the latter, and led a force of three legions with distinction during the civil war that followed, serving in Sicily and North Africa. This useful political alliance boosted Pompey's reputation, and by 81 BC he was being hailed as Imperator by his men—and "the teenage butcher" by his critics. It was Sulla who added the cognomen Magnus ("the Great"). Following the political split between Pompey and Sulla, the young general campaigned against Sulla's forces in Spain, and by 71 BC he had subdued the province in the name of the Roman Senate.

Following his celebratory consulship (70 BC) he was given the monumental task of ridding the Mediterranean of pirates—a task he performed brilliantly during a two-

Left: A marble bust of Pompey "the Great," veteran Roman general, influential statesmen, and great military and political rival of Julius Caesar.

Below: The blood-stained tunic worn by Pompey, shown to his family after his death (in a detail from a 17th century Flemish tapestry illustrating the life of the Roman general).

Above: The Assassination of Pompey "the Great," a 19th century painting by Bandini.

year-long campaign, working his way east from the Pillars of Hercules (Gibraltar) to the coast of Judea. Next he was sent east to fight King Mithridates of Pontus, in which he was succeesful, and in 63 BC he extended the campaign to insure Roman control over much of the Middle East. However, the Roman establishment resented Pompey's success, and so his solution was to form a political triumvirate with Crassus and Caesar. Between them the men maintained a grip on the Roman political establishment for a decade, despite the death of Crassus in Parthia (54 BC) and the growing divide between Caesar and Pompey.

Matters reached a head in 49 BC when, after conquering Gaul, Caesar refused to disband his armies. Instead, he "crossed the Rubicon" and initiated a civil war between himself and Pompey, who fought on behalf of the Senate. Pompey abandoned Rome to Caesar and withdrew to Greece.

There the rivals fought two major battles the following year, at Dyrrhachium and Pharsalus. Both proved to be Pompeian defeats, and so Pompey was forced to flee to Egypt. Caesar pursued, only to find that Pompey had been slain by assassins— a shabby end for a man who spent his life fighting for the good of the Roman Republic.

Porus
(reigned 340–317 BC)
Indian King

King Priam
Trojan War
King of Troy (mythological)

Porus is said to have given Alexander the Great his hardest battle, at the Hydaspes River in 326 BC, in which heavy losses were suffered on both sides. So impressed was Alexander that he awarded Porus a neighboring kingdom. Porus campaigned alongside Alexander throughout India and continued to rule for several years after his departure until being assassinated in 317 BC.

In Homer's description of the Trojan War, King Priam escorted Hector's father into the Achaean camp and begged Achilles to return Hector's body. Moved by his plea, Achilles agreed to the return of the corpse and also granted an eleven-day truce. In other accounts, Priam is murdered by Achilles' son, Neoptolemus.

Above: The head of King Priam of Troy, from the eastern pediment of the temple of Aegina, Greece, c.490 BC.

Ptolemy I "Soter"

(367-283 BC)
Macedonian General and King of Egypt

Ptolemy was the son of Arsinoe, who was once a mistress of King Philip of Macedon. Consequently, it was claimed that Ptolemy was the king's illegitimate son, which would make him a half-brother of Alexander "the Great." He was brought up in the Macedonian court, and became a close childhood friend of the younger Alexander. He accompanied Alexander on his conquest of the Persian Empire, and soon became one of the Macedonian king's most trusted generals. He played a leading part in Alexander's later campaigns in Bactria and India, and in 324 BC his marriage to the Persian princess Atacama helped strengthen the bonds linking Alexander to his new Persian throne.

When Alexander "the Great" died in 323, Ptolemy called a meeting of the senior Macedonian commanders, and they divided Alexander's empire up between them. As a result, he became the Satrap (governor) of Egypt, ruling in the name of Alexander's retarded child successor, Alexander IV and his regent, General Perdiccas. However, Ptolemy was determined to forge his own path, and he soon formed an alliance against Perdiccas and others among the other Alexandrian commanders. In 321 BC Perdiccas responded by invading Egypt, but his attempts to force a crossing of the Nile were thwarted by Ptolemy. Perdiccas was then assassinated, and Ptolemy turned down the offer to replace him as regent, preferring to strengthen his own power base in Egypt.

During the "Successor Wars" that followed Ptolemy expanded his frontiers by conquering Judea, Syria, and Cyprus. In 312 BC he formed an alliance with Seleucus and defeated his main rival, Demetrius, son of Antigones, at the Battle of Gaza. The following year a peace was concluded in which Ptolemy ceded Syria in the confirmation of his control over Judea. The war resumed after the assassination of Alexander IV, and Ptolemy campaigned unsuccessfully against Antigonus in Greece and Cyprus. He then repulsed an Antigonid attack on Egypt, and relieved Rhodes, which was held by his ally Demetrius. This action led to the bestowing of the title "Soter" (Savior). The war simmered on in Syria until Ptolemy's death, but by that time his hold over Egypt had become unassailable, and the royal dynasty he created continued to rule Egypt for another 250 years.

Below: Ptolemy I "Soter," the Satrap of Alexandria, depicted on a 3rd century BC silver tetradrachma coin wearing a headress made from the skin of an elephant.

Publius Appius Claudius Pulcher
(c288-247 BC)
Republican Roman General

Claudius commanded the Roman fleet during the First Punic War. He lost the Battle of Drepana in 249 BC, supposedly for ignoring a bad omen; the sacred chickens had refused to eat. He was recalled to Rome, tried for incompetence, and fined. He died soon afterwards, possibly by committing suicide.

Left: Publius Claudius "Pulcher," a less than successful Roman naval commander during the first Punic War, who was ultimately made a scapegoat for Rome's lack of success at sea.

Qin Shi Huang
259 -210 BC
Chinese King

King of the Chinese state of Qin and then first emperor of a unified China from 221 to 210 BC, Qin started huge building projects across China, including a national road system, the fortifications later known as the Great Wall, and the city-sized mausoleum guarded by the life-sized Terracotta Army.

Right: Quin Shi Huang is best known as the Chinese ruler who first designed the Great Wall of China.

Quintus Fabius Maximus

(275-203 BC)
Republican Roman General

Little is known about the young Fabius, although he came from a well-respected Roman patrician family, and several of his ancestors had served as consuls. He almost certainly gained his first military experience during the First Punic War (264-241 BC), and when peace came he concentrated on his political career, rising steadily up the Roman political ladder. He was elected as consul in 233 BC, and served in the post a second time five years later. In 218 BC he took part in an embassy to Carthage that formally declared war between the two rival cities following the breakdown of talks.

The Roman military disasters of 218 and 217 BC led to his election as dictator in the summer of 217 BC—charged with masterminding the war against Hannibal. He realized that the Roman armies and commanders lacked the experience needed to guarantee victory against Hannibal, so he devised a completely new set of tactics to counter the Carthaginian threat. Fabius refused to offer battle, and instead he tried to wear his enemy down by conducting a lengthy war of attrition. Roman troops would harass Carthaginian foraging parties and interrupt Hannibal's supply lines, while a "scorched earth" policy would deny Rome's enemy of provisions. These "Fabian" tactics proved successful.

Unfortunately the Romans soon tired of this inglorious but effective strategy, and Fabius' deputy Mincius almost fell into one of Hannibal's traps before his commander was able to rescue him. In 217 BC Fabius ceded his dictatorship, and the new consuls Paullus and Varro immediately reversed the Fabian policy, and sought battle. The result was the Battle of Cannae, where the Roman army was all but annihilated. The wisdom of the Fabian policy had been ably demonstrated, and so in 215 and 214 BC Fabius was re-elected as dictator. As a result Hannibal's army was effectively neutralized and, while it remained in southern Italy, other Roman armies—most notably the one commanded by Scipio Africanus—successfully managed to take the war to the enemy in Spain and North Africa. Unfortunately, the "Shield of Rome" died before Rome's final victory over Carthage was achieved.

Radagaisus
(c. 405 AD)
King of the Goths

In 405 AD Radagaisus led a Gothic horde into Northern Italy, having marched across the Alps. After plundering the Po valley he continued southwards into modern Tuscany, until in 406 AD he encountered Stilicho's small Roman army outside Florentia (now Florence). Despite their numerical advantage the Goths were defeated, and Radagaisus was captured and executed.

Ramses II "the Great"
(c.1303-1213 BC)
Egyptian Pharaoh

Ramses II (also transcribed as Ramesses or Rameses) is generally regarded as the most successful ruler of Ancient Egypt. He was born around 1303 BC, although the exact date is unrecorded. When he was fourteen the prince was

Right: Pharaoh Ramses II shown wearing the double crown of Upper and Lower Egypt, and the crook and flail symbols of Egyptian kingship.
Below: A doorway in the temple of Medinet Habu, with a relief of the victory of Ramses II over the Sea Peoples.

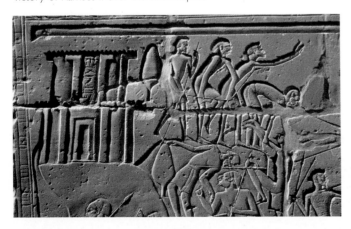

Above: The façade of the great Temple of Ramses II at Abu Simbel, dominated by four great statues of the seated Pharaohs.
Right: Ramses II depicted wielding an ax and grabbing the hair of three symbolic captives—a Libyan, a Numidian, and a Syrian.

named as the successor to his father, Pharaoh Seti I, and he eventually succeeded to the Egyptian throne in 1279 BC. Ramses, the third member of his dynasty, was in his early twenties when he became Pharaoh, and retained his control of the kingdom for two thirds of a century—making him the longest-reigning ruler of Ancient Egypt.

His achievements were legendary, having been linked by the Greek writer Heroditus to the mythical god-like Egyptian Pharaoh Sesostris, who reputedly conquered the entire known world. He was also believed to be the pharaoh who opposed the flight of the Israelites, as described in the Book of Exodus, although there is no historic basis for this long-discredited assumption. He is known to have had several wives, the most famous of which was Nefratiti, whose name means "Beautiful Companion." She married the pharaoh when she was just fifteen, and remained his most important wife for more than two decades. Nefratiti bore Ramses at least six children, although scholars now estimate that the total number of his progeny numbered anywhere from 40 to 110.

Apart from his military achievements, Ramses was best remembered for the buildings he commissioned. He established a new capital city in the Nile Delta—Pi-Ramesses—which became the center for his administration and a base for his campaigns against the Hittites. The city was established on the ruins of Avaris, a city that had once belonged to the neighboring Hyksos people before they were conquered by Ramses' army. It was already known as a religious center before the establishment of the new city, but Ramses turned the site into one of the most important religious sites in Egypt, at the center of which was the Temple of Seti. It was here that Ramses was supposedly able to harness the power of the gods Set, Re, Horus, and Amun to help him further the greatness of his kingdom. The temple also became the place where the pharaoh's martial deeds were recorded for posterity in hieroglyphs.

Below: The mummified remains of the Pharaoh Ramses II, approximately ninety years old when he died.
Following page: Ramses II, wearing the blue crown of Lower Egypt, and receiving ankh, the symbol of life—a bas relief carving from the 19th dynasty.

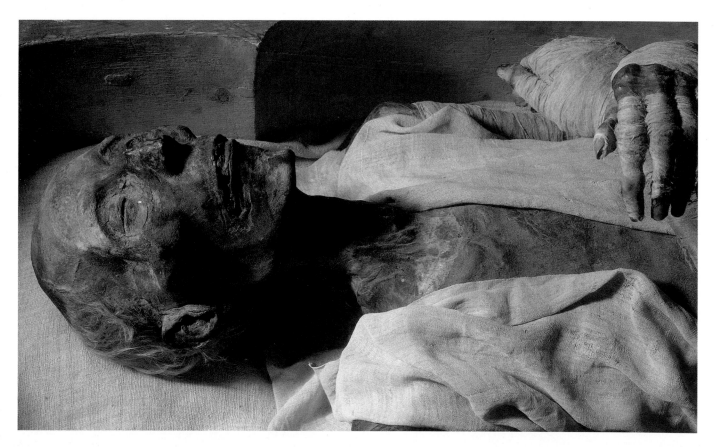

One of the most significant of these was his defeat of the "Sea Peoples," the maritime raiders who had been harassing the Egyptian coast and interrupting Egyptian maritime trade. In the second year of his reign Ramses fought a sea battle with these raiders and pirates, and inflicted a decisive defeat upon them. He later incorporated the surviving pirates into his army, by which stage they were known as the Sherden people, renowned for their ferocity and marital skill. Ramses also conducted several campaigns up the Nile, reclaiming territory that had been lost by his ancestors, and re-establishing Egyptian control over the river as far as the edge of the Nubian desert.

However, Ramses' most important military achievement was his great victory over the Hittites at Kadesh, fought in 1274 BC in what is now modern Syria. His war against the Hittites began the previous year when the Egyptian army advanced through what is now Israel into the fertile Bekaa valley, now in Lebanon. He decided to seize the Hittite stronghold of Kadesh, but instead he encountered the main Hittite army, commanded by King Muwatalli II, who managed to ambush the Egyptian advance guard. It was claimed that the Hittites "were more numerous than grains of sand on the beach."

Ramses had already divided his army into four commands (called Ra, Amun, Set, and Ptah), and it was the Ra force that was being ambushed. Ramses led the rest of the army into the fray, spearheaded by the Amun division. After a bloody fight the Hittite chariots were driven back, across the River Orontes, but King Muwatalli sent in his reserve of 1,000 chariots, and the fight was renewed. According to Egyptian accounts, the pharaoh's division was cut off, and might well have been overrun were it not for a counterattack by a small Egyptian reserve. This proved too much for the Hittites, whose army

Left: A red granite statue of Ramses II, flanked by the Egyptian god Amon, and his consort, the goddess Mut..

Left: The statue of Ramses II with his daughter Bentana at his feet in the courtyard of the Temple of Karnax, in Luxor, Egypt.
Above: The granite head of the Pharaoh Ramses II, on a 19th dynasty piece from the temple of Luxor, Egypt.

broke and fled the field.

Ramses had certainly won the battle, but he had effectively lost the war, as his losses were too severe for him to maintain control of the region. He led his army south, and spent the next few years on the defensive in Canaan, protecting his existing provinces from Hittite invasion. However, Ramses had proved himself in battle, and thanks to the inscriptions of the Temple of Seti it would be him rather than King Muwatalli who would be seen as the victor of Kadesh. A peace treaty was eventually signed with the Hittites in 1258 BC, and Ramses devoted himself to improving the prosperity of his kingdom.

Ramses III
(1186-1155 BC)
Egyptian Pharaoh

The last great New Kingdom king, Ramses defeated the Sea Peoples but the cost of numerous battles weakened Egypt's finances. Ramses began the reconstruction of the Temple of Khonsu and completed the Temple of Medinet Habu. Later, a conspiracy was uncovered against Ramses which led to many executions. Ramses was succeeded by his son Ramses IV.

Previous page: Ramesses III, making an offering of lotus and papyrus to the gods, from a limestone relief from the Temple of Medinet Habu, Egypt.
Above: Ramses III, shown holding a ceremonial stave bearing the head of the god Amun-Re in the form of a ram.

Above: The peristyle façade of the Temple of Ramses III at Karnak, viewed from its courtyard, dominated by statues of the Pharaoh as the god Osiris.
Below: Ramses III offering gifts to the creator-god Atum, while holding an ankh symbol in his left hand, from a limestone relief from the tomb of Ramses III in the Valley of the Kings.

Marcus Atilius Regulus
(c310-250 BC)
Republican Roman Admiral and Statesman

One of the commanders of the Roman fleet that destroyed the Carthaginian fleet at Cape Ecnomus, Regulus suffered defeat in the Battle of Tunis in 255BC and was taken prisoner. It is claimed that he returned to Rome to negotiate peace for the Carthaginians but he advised the Senate against this and was executed on his return to Carthage.

Above: Marcus Atilius Regulus advising his fellow Romans not to make peace with the Carthaginians, in an early 16th century fresco by Jacopo Ripanda.

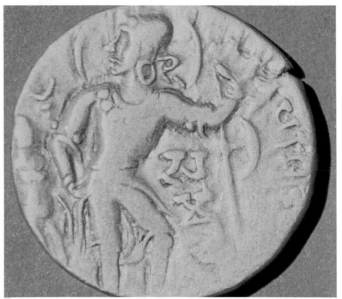

Samudragupta
(335-380 AD)
Indian Gupta Emperor

Samudragupta is considered one of the great military geniuses in Indian history. The details of his extraordinary military career are recorded in a series of stone pillars, set

Above: Indian gold dinar coins from the reigns of Samudragupta (335-375), Kumaragupta I (415-454), and Chandragupta I (320-335), from the collection of the National Museum of India in Delhi.

up in Allahabad to celebrate his achievements. His predecessor Chandragupta I married into the Lichchhavi dynasty, which allowed him to add the area encompassing the modern state of Bahar to his domains. A power struggle followed his death in 335 AD, but eventually he was succeeded by Samandragupta, a younger son who vanquished his elder brothers to claim the throne. He inherited a fairly small Gupta Empire that encompassed much of the Ganges Basin, but he had plans to dramatically expand its borders. He began by conquering the small kingdoms of Shichchhatra and Padmavati, followed by the larger region of Ahichchhatra , south of the Ganges. All these additions to his empire strengthened its geographical position in Northern India.

Samudragupta then moved south into Madhya Pradesh, and then turned east to conquer Orissa, on the coast of the Bay of Bengal. From the Orissa city of Ganjam he led his army south to besiege and capture the cities of Vishakapatnam and Nellore, and the Godavari and Krishna provinces of what is now the state of Andhra Pradesh. Beyond Nellore lay Kancheepuram, the capital of the Pallava dynasty, which ruled Southern India in the 4th century AD. Rather than continuing on Samudragupta wisely consolidated his gains, installing subsidiary rulers in his newly conquered provinces.

Later campaigns were aimed at strengthening his empire, and in quelling insurgency. He defeated the

Left and Below: More gold dinars dating from the Samudragupta era in Indian politics.

Arjunayanas tribe of Northern India, and besieged and captured their capital of Maduras. Similar treatment was afforded the Malwas and Yaudheyas tribes in Central India, and he protected the borders against the Scythians (known as the "Saka") to the east and the Kushana of what is now Afghanistan. By the time of his death in 380 AD Samudragupta's empire encompassed all of what is now Pakistan and Northern India, from the Himalayas to the Narmada River, the traditional boundary between Northern and Southern India. In his lifetime Samudragupta was called "King of Kings." and modern historians have dubbed him "The Napoleon of India."

Sargon II
(reigned 722-705 BC)
King of Assyria

Sargon fought a number of successful campaigns against the Egyptians and the Urartians, and he took Babylon after a siege. Sargon was proclaimed King of Babylon in 710 BC thus restoring the dual monarchy of Assyria and Babylon, but he was killed in 705 BC during a campaign against the Cimmerians.

Right: Sargon II, King of Assyria, with an emissary—from an 8th century AD relief from the Palace of Sargon II, Dur Sarrukin. Iraq.

brothers in the army. David killed Goliath, the Philistine champion, with a sling-shot and thus the Philistines were again defeated. However, Saul became jealous of the praise heaped on David for killing Goliath. He tried several times to kill David but the shepherd boy eventually fled. Saul pursued David and David had the opportunity of killing Saul, but did not.

Eventually David allied himself with the Philistines and returned to meet the Israelites once again in battle. Saul marched out to meet the Philistine army at Gilboa but before hostilities commenced the ghost of Samuel told Saul that he would lose the battle and die. Tthe following day the army of the Israelites was

Saul
(1028-1015 BC)
King of the Israelites

Above: "Saul attacking David," from an early 17th century painting by Giovanni Francesco Barbieri Guercino.

Below: David showing Saul the corner of his robe, thereby demonstrating his restraint in only cutting the cloth rather than Saul.

In the Book of Samuel, Saul is described as the son of a man named Kish and a member of the Benjamin tribe. There are several accounts of how Saul became king, but as leader of the Israelites Saul managed to throw off Philistine rule when his small army, although heavily outnumbered, defeated the Philistines in battle.

When another Philistine force returned to face the Israelites it was suggested that the battle should be resolved by a combat between champions, Saul appointed David, a young shepherd boy visiting his elder

Publius Cornelius Scipio "Africanus"
(236-185 BC)
Republican Roman General

Perhaps the greatest general of the Roman Republic after Julius Caesar, Scipio earned the cognomen "Africanus" after defeating Hannibal, a feat that placed the Roman commander in the pantheon of great ancient military commanders. The Scipio family were a branch of the Cornelii family, one of the great aristocratic houses of Republican Rome, and Scipio's father (also called Publius Cornelius Scipio) had served as a Roman consul. It was later claimed that Scipio served in the army against Hannibal, and survived the disastrous Roman defeats at the Trebbia and Cannae. In 211 BC his father and uncle were killed in battle in Spain while fighting against the Carthaginian general Hasdrubal, the brother of Hannibal. The grieving son immediately ran for public office, and on being elected he was named proconsul and was given command of the remnants of the Roman army in Spain.

In 210 BC he arrived to take control of his late father's army in 210 BC, at that time encamped north of the River Ebro, which was then the border of Carthaginian territory. He soon discovered that the able Hasdrubal shared command with his brother Mago, and also with another Carthaginian commander, Hasdrubal Gisco. Scipio realized that coordina-

tion between the three forces was difficult. In 209 BC he took advantage of this by striking southwards down the coast to the city of New Carthage (now Cartagena), the capital of Carthaginian Spain. By securing

Above: Scipio "Africanus," the celebrated Roman general who defeated Hannibal at the Battle of Zama (202 BC).

control of the city Scipio gained a useful port, and a base of operations

139

against the Carthaginians.

In the spring of 208 BC he marched west towards the head of the Guadalquivir River, where he attacked and defeated Hasdrubal at the Battle of Baecula. Scipio's aim was to defeat Hasdrubal's force before it could be reinforced by the other two Carthaginian armies, so he launched a costly frontal attack to pin down the enemy, while sending his cavalry around the enemy's flank to attack them in the rear. The result was a spirited victory, but Hasdrubal managed to withdraw his battered army, and he eventually marched it

Above: Fire in the camp of Syphax—a detail from a 17th century leather panel depicting the life of Scipio Africanus.

out of the theater completely, in an effort to reinforce his brother Hannibal's army in Italy. Hasdrubal's army was cornered and defeated at

Above: One of the scenes depicting "The Continence of Scipio." This by 15th century artist Apollinio di Giovanni (see next page).
Right: "Scipio's Dream," by Cicero (106-43 BC) shows Scipio in bed dreaming of Rome and Carthage in heavenly spheres, with his father, grandfather, and himself in the Milky Way.

the Battle of the Metaurus the following year.

Meanwhile, Scipio had other problems. The armies of Mago and Hasdrubal Gisco had managed to unite, and the two sides began a campaign of maneuver in what is now Andalusia, which ended in the Battle of Illipa, fought near the modern city of Seville in 206 BC. This time Scipio outflanked his more numerous opponents and fell on the Carthaginian army from its flank. The result was a brilliant victory that marked the end of Carthaginian rule in Spain. He concluded the campaign by capturing the last remaining Carthaginian stronghold of Gades (now Cadiz), then returned to Rome, where he was feted as a hero.

In 205 BC the thirty-one-year-old Scipio was elected as consul, and despite his demands to take the war to the gates of Carthage the Senate ordered him to Sicily, where he raised an army and drove the Carthaginians from the island. This disrupted the communications between Hannibal in Calabria (the "toe of Italy") and Carthage (in modern Tunisia). By 204 BC Scipio had formed his Sicilian force into a highly motivated and well-trained Roman

army, supported by its own fleet. While the Senate debated what to do next, Scipio seized the initiative and landed his army near Utica, an African port northwest of Carthage. Although forced to abandon the siege of the port by the advance of a large relief force, Scipio established himself in a fortified camp and waited. When the opportunity came he launched a surprise assault on the enemy camp and routed the Carthaginian army.

After some political maneuvering to strip Carthage of its Numidian allies, Scipio launched his campaign against Carthage. Hannibal was recalled to take command of the Carthaginian army, and the two forces

eventually met at Zama in October 202 BC. Hannibal hoped to use his superior numbers to outflank the Romans while his war elephants disrupted the enemy front, but Scipio's men drove off the elephants, which rampaged through the Carthaginian center. Scipio launched his infantry in a counter-attack. Meanwhile, his cavalry managed to defeat their Carthaginian counterparts, then fell upon the flanks of the Carthaginian infantry. The day ended in a resounding Roman victory.

When peace was declared Scipio returned to Rome in triumph, and after a decade as a civilian he retuned to the army in 190 BC. Alongside his

Above: Feted as a hero following his victories over Carthage, Scipio shows great continence (restraint) in handing back a "gift," the Princess Lucretia, to Allucius, to whom she was betrothed (from a painting by Frederico di Madrazo).

brother he defeated the Seleucid king Antiochus III at the Battle of Magnesia. On his return to Rome his enemies pursued a legal vendetta against him, accusing him of corruption. Although his popularity helped insure his acquittal, he retired from public life, and died five years later. It was an unnecessarily sordid end for a man who defeated Rome's greatest enemy.

Seleucus I "Nicator"

(358-280 BC)
Macedonian General and
King of Seleucia

Seleucid was the son of Antiochus, one of Alexander the Great's principal generals. In 333 BC he served with Alexander during his campaigns in Bactria, Sogdia, and Afghanistan, and he distinguished himself during Alexander's invasion of India in 326 BC. In the partition of the empire that followed Alexander's death Seleucus served with Perdiccas, the regent of Alexander's son. However, five years later Seleucus murdered the regent, acting on behalf of Ptolemy, with whom he formed an alliance. In 321 BC Seleucus became the governor of Babylonia, although his control over the region was not secured until 312 BC, when his neighbor and rival Antigonus was defeated by Ptolemy.

Duirng the years that followed Seleucus expanded his domains by conquering Persia and Media, and by 305 BC his new-found Seleucid Empire stretched as far as India and Central Asia. At that point he assumed the rank of king, and established his new capital at Seleucia, on the River Tigris. A treaty with the Indian King Sandrocottus secured his eastern borders, allowing Seleucus to concentrate his efforts on other matters, such as the founding of new cities. He is

Right: Bronze bust of Seleucus I "Nicator," King of Seleucia, from the Villa dei Oisoni at Herculaneaum.

Telentius anthorius

reputed to have built no fewer than nine Seleucias, sixteen Antiochs, and six Laodiceas. The capture of his rival Demetrius I, the son of his old enemy Antigonus, greatly enhanced the prestige of Seleucus, since it meant that of all his successor rivals, apart from his Ptolemaic Egyptian allies, his only enemy remaining in the fray was Lysimachus, who controlled Macedonia, Thrace, and Asia Minor.

War between the two successor kings was inevitable, and so in 281 BC Seleucus invaded Lysimachus' provinces in Asia Minor. The two armies met at the Battle of Corupedium, which resulted in victory for Seleucus and the death of Lysimachus. Seleucus immediately marched east to take control of the rest of Lysimachus' territories, which meant that, apart from Egypt, Seleucus now controlled all the lands once conquered by Alexander the Great. He was therefore at the height of his power when he was assassinated by the agents of Ptolemy's successor.

Left: "The Story of Seleucus," from a 15th century manuscript, describing how the Syrian king's son, Antiochus, came near to death over his love of his stepmother.

Sennacherib
(705-681 BC)
King of Assyria

Septimus Severus
(146-211 AD)
Roman General and Emperor

Sennacherib came to power following the death of his father, Sargon II. He suppressed several rebellions in Babylon and a rebellion in Judah, which concluded with the unsuccessful siege of Jerusalem. Sennacherib developed Nineveh as the leading city of the empire, extending its fortifications and constructing the first ever aqueduct.

Above: Assyrian slingers—from a 7th century BC limestone relief in the Palace of Ashurbanipal in Nineveh.

Septimus Severus was raised in Leptis Magna (now Libya), and although of noble birth his father was of Liby-Phoenecian origin. His mother was a member of the Fulvius dynasty, one of the most influential families in Rome. Consequently, Severus was brought up in the mainstream of Imperial Roman politics, and when he was

Above: A Roman marble bust of the soldier and Emperor Septimus Severus, c.200 AD.

twenty-six he became a senator. He also served as a soldier, although the details of his service are sketchy. In 190 AD Severus became a consul, and the Emperor Commodus appointed him as commander of the Roman frontier garrison of Pannonia (which comprised most of modern Hungary). When Commodus was murdered in late 192 AD a power struggle followed, which became known as

"The Year of the Five Emperors" (193 AD). Severus was with his army at Carnuntum (in modern Austria), and when his troops declared their support for him he declared himself an Imperial candidate, and marched on Rome. That summer he had the current claimant killed, and took possession of the capital without opposition. However, he still had two rivals—Pescennius Niger in Syria and

Above: The Emperor Septimus Severus and Caracalla—from a late 18th century painting by Jean Baptiste Greuze.

Clodius Albinus in Britannia. Severus made a deal with Albinus, insuring his support in return for a claim to his succession. He then marched east to confront Niger, and the two armies met at Issus, on the southeastern coast of Asia Minor. Niger's army was crushed, and shortly afterwards Severus' rival was killed while attempting to flee from Syria. When Albinus revolted, Severus marched into Gaul, and in 197 AD his remaining rival was defeated and killed in the resulting Battle of Lugdunum (Lyon).

Septimus Severus was a soldier emperor. He led his legions on campaign against the Parthians in 197 AD, which ensured that Mesopotamia became part of the Roman Empire. Then, in 208 AD, he traveled to Roman Britain, which was threatened by incursions from the north. He campaigned extensively in what is now Scotland, and although he was never able to subdue the Caledonii, he managed to prevent raids across Britannia's northern frontier. He was preparing a fresh campaign in early 211 AD when he fell ill, and he died in the legionary fortress of York. He was duly succeeded by his son Caracalla.

Below: The triple arch built by Septimius Severus to mark the entrance to the Roman town of Lambesi (now Tazoult), Algeria..

Shapur I
(reigned 241-272 AD)
King of Sassanid Persia

Above: The triumph of Shapur I, King of Sassanid Persia, over the Emperor Valerian—from a rock bas relief beneath the necropolis of Naqsh-e-Rustam, Iran.

The son of the founder of the Sassanid dynasty, Shapur succeeded his father in 241 AD, and after campaigning in modern-day Iraq he went to war with the Romans. In 260 AD his troops captured the Emperor Valerian near Edessa, although a further war with the Palmyrans prevented Shapur from exploiting his success before his death.

Lucius Flavius Silva

(c.73 AD)
Roman General

While serving as the Roman military governor of Judea, Silva was faced with a major Jewish revolt. He participated in the siege and capture of Jerusalem (70 AD), and then cornered and besieged the rebels in their hilltop fortress of Masada (73 AD). When Silva's victory was inevitable the defenders took their own lives rather than face his legionaries.

Sima Yi

(179-251 AD)
Chinese Han General and Strategist

Sima Yi is best known for his defense of the post-Han dynasty state of Cao Wei in the face of Zhuge Liang's "Northern Expeditions" (228-234 AD), although he is also celebrated as a grand strategist who paved the way for the foundation of the Jin Dynasty by his grandson Sima Yan.

Right: Sima Yi was a key general and statesman of the Wei Kingdom, who played a major role during the era of the Three Kingdoms.

Spartacus
(c.120-70 BC)
Leader of Slave Revolt

Spartacus was most probably a Thracian, who once served as a mercenary auxiliary in the Republican Roman army. It was suggested by Roman historians that he joined the Roman army but deserted, and became a robber. When captured he was saved by his military skills, and he was sold into slavery as a gladiator. There had been other slave revolts during the period of the late Roman Republic, but the worst of them—dubbed the Third Servile War—was instigated by Spartacus. In 73 BC Spartacus and seventy fellow gladiators escaped from the gladiatorial school of Lentulus Batiatus. The escapees took refuge on the slopes of Mount Vesuvius, near modern Naples, and they soon attracted other runaway slaves.

An inexperienced Roman legion was sent to round up the fugitives, but Spartacus bypassed the Roman lines and then launched a surprise attack on their camp. The Romans were slaughtered, and this success led to a widespread revolt throughout the province of Capua, as thousands of slaves killed their masters and joined Spartacus' army. He spent several months training his recruits, and then used these men to defeat two more Roman forces that were sent south to crush the revolt. By early 72 BC he had some 120,000 followers, including women and children. Spartacus

decided to seek sanctuary in Gaul, although a splinter group remained behind. He marched north to Picenum, defeating two Roman consuls, and at Mutina he defeated a third army, commanded by the governor of Cisalpine Gaul.

Then he inexplicably headed

Above: A gladiator killing a Christian—in a detail from the mosaic pavement of a 3rd century AD Roman villa at Curium in Cyprus.

south again, brushing aside a force commanded by Crassus to reach the Straits of Messina by the end of the year. A deal with local pirates fell through, leaving Spartacus without a

Below: Gladiators armed with whips, spears, and bare hands are locked in combat with wild animals (from a Roman bas relief).

means of escape. By now Crassus had hemmed him in with eight legions, and in 71 BC Spartacus was decisively defeated and probably killed. Many of those slaves who survived were crucified, as a warning to others, while

Pompey rounded up the few remaining fugitives still at large. Thanks to a movie produced in 1960, Spartacus is now one of the best-known figures in ancient history.

Stilicho

(359-408 AD)
Late Roman General

Stilicho was born in Germany, the offspring of a vandal father and a Roman mother. He joined the army of the Eastern Roman Emperor Theodosius I, and clearly he earned the support of his ruler, since in 384 AD Stilicho was sent as the Roman envoy to the court of the Sassanid Persian King Shapur III. On his return he was promoted to the rank of general, and charged with defending the Eastern Roman frontier against the incursions of the Goths. After the assassination of the Western Roman Emperor Valentian II, Stilicho's troops played a major part in the civil wars that followed, and helped to insure Theodosius' victory over his Western rivals at the Battle of Frigidus (394 AD).

Theodosius may have reunited the Empire, but his death the following year plunged it back into chaos. Stilicho acted as the guardian of Theodosius' eleven-year-old son Honorius, but the Empire was soon divided again, with Honorius and his regent governing its Western portion. In effect, Stilicho became the *de facto* head of the Western Roman Empire. Although Stilicho was a highly capable general, he lacked the experience to avoid entanglement in the politics of the two Imperial courts. Alaric of the Visigoths had served as Stilicho's ally in 394 AD, but the barbarian's betrayal by the new Eastern Emperor Arcadius led to a Gothic invasion of Greece. Stilicho was asked to intervene, but political considerations prevented him from calling on military support from the East. However, in 397 Stilicho defeated Alaric in Macedonia, forcing the Visigoths to withdraw to the north.

Stilicho then campaigned against the Vandals in North Africa, but by 402 the Visigoths were threatening Italy, so the general was recalled to defend Honorius' capital at Ravenna. Stilicho again defeated Alaric, at Pollentia (402 AD) and Verona (403 AD), forcing the Visigoths to

Left: The Romanized general Stilicho and his wife, in an ivory diptych dating from the early 5th century AD.

withdraw, and two years later he repelled another Gothic invasion led by Radagaisus after defeating him outside the modern city of Florence. However, Honorius' other advisors were jealous of Stilicho's successes, and in the summer of 406 AD they orchestrated his disgrace and imprisonment on trumped-up charges. Stilicho was executed two years later. In Stilicho, Rome lost its last protector, and two years after his execution the once-great city was sacked by Alaric and his Visigoths.

Sudas

(c.15th century BC)
Indian Bharata King

Sudas was a semi-mythical Indian ruler of the "Aryan" Bharata (or Trtsu) people mentioned in the Hindu *Rig Veda* scriptures. These record that he fought in the Battle of the Ten Kings, repelling an invasion of his Punjabi kingdom by a confederation of rival tribes.

Lucius Cornelius Sulla

(138-78BC)
Republican Roman General and Statesman

Born into a poor but patrician family, Sulla learned his military trade under Gaius Marius, and in 107 BC he participated in the Jugarthine War in North Africa. Victory was guaranteed when Sulla captured the Numidian king, an achievement that greatly enhanced his reputation in Rome. From 97-93 BC Sulla served as a governor in Asia Minor, where he defeated the Aemenian King Tigranes "the Great" before returning to Rome in triumph. During the Social War fought between Roman and rebel Italian citizens Sulla demonstrated his military prowess and bravery, particularly during the siege of Nola, where he won "The Grass Crown," Rome's highest military honor. However, he also severed his friendship with Gaius Marius, as both men were on opposite sides of a growing political divide. When Marius seized control of Rome Sulla fled to join his legions, and then marched north to reconquer the city from the Marians.

Sulla then led his army into Greece, where he campaigned against Mithridates of Pontus, but during his absence in 87 BC Marius returned from exile and recaptured Rome. Although Marius died shortly afterwards his populist allies still controlled the city, so Sulla hastily brought his Greek campaign to a conclusion, capturing Athens, then marching north to crush the far larger Pontic army at Chaeronea (86 BC). While he was still consolidating his hold on Greece a Marian army appeared, which Sulla encouraged to defect to his side. Using these reinforcements he inflicted another defeat on Mithridates at Orchomenos, thereby winning the war and ensuring Roman control over the Aegean basin.

He was now free to return to Italy. In 82 BC his army landed at Brindisium and marched on Rome. He met a combined army of Marian supporters and Samnite rebels at the Colline Gate, and with the help of the young commanders Pompey and Crassus he won a stunning victory, and secured control of Rome. Sulla was duly appointed dictator, and as such he waged a reign of terror on Marius' supporters, during which thousands of Romans were killed. Then, in 81 BC he relinquished his office, and retired to his country estates, where he died three years later.

Left: A detail of a Roman statue showing Lucus Cornelius Sulla, dating from the early 1st century BC.

Sun Quan (also Sun Chian)
(182-252 AD)
Chinese Wu Emperor

The founder of the Eastern Wu Empire, Sun Quan forged his own state on the Yangtse River, defeating rival warlord Cao Cao at the Battle of Red Cliffs (208 AD), and the powerful ruler Liu Bei at the Battle of Xiaoting (222 AD). He was perhaps the most successful of all the founders of the Three Kingdoms.

Right: Sun Quan, a Chinese warlord of the Wu Kingdom during the Three Kingdoms period.

兵者，国之大事，死生之地，存亡之道，不可不察也

中国邮政

20 分

CHINA

1995-26   (5—1) T

Sun Tzu

(c.544–496 BC)
Chinese General and Author

Sun Tzu is he author of *The Art of War*, an influential book on military strategy still widely read in modern times. Sun Tzu was a landless Chinese aristocrat, hired as a mercenary after completing his book, apparently helping the king of the Wu gain prominence over the Chu.

Left: Sun Tzu, renowned strategists, whose methods of conducting war are still studied today.

Surena

(c.84-52 BC)
Parthian General

Surena was a renowned cavalry commander who fought in the battle for Seleucia in 54 BC and reinstated Orodes to the Arsacid throne. He led a force of horse archers and Cataphracts against the Romans at the Battle of Carrhae in 53 BC, causing their defeat. Unfortunately, Orodes grew to fear his erstwhile ally and had him executed.

Theodosius I "the Great"

(347-395AD)
Roman Emperor

Flavius Theodosius was born in Hispania and served under his father, the general Theodosius. He successfully fought the Sarmatians of Moesia but after his father's execution he retired to Cauca in 376 AD. Gratian appointed Theodosius ruler of the Eastern Empire following the death of Valens in 378 AD. Theodosius fought a successful campaign against Goth invaders along the Danube and later went on to fight and smash the usurper Maximus (388 AD) following the death of Gratian.

In 389 AD Theodosius granted the western part of the empire to Valentian II. Theodosius was forced, in 394AD, to lead his army back to Italy after general Arbogast murdered Valentian. Theodosius' army, composed mainly of Goths, faced Arbogast at the River Frigidus. The battle was fought over two days; the first day went to the rebels, but after Theodosius reorganized his force, Arbogast's army was routed on the second day. Several days later Arbogast committed suicide.

Theodosius ended his days in Milan where he died of dropsy in 395. An inventive and capable leader and a gifted general, Theodosius was the last emperor able to control both the Eastern and Western Roman Empire, where his reign brought a brief period of harmony to the Empire.

Above: A detail from the relief of an obelisk of Theodosius I "the Great." showing the emperor and his courtiers at a race held in the hippodrome of Byzantium.

Themistocles
(514–449 BC)
Greek Admiral and Statesman

Little is known of Themistocles' early life, other than that he was born in Athens c.514 BC to a modest family, He fought at Marathon in 490 BC and following the death of Miltiades became one of the leading political and military figures in Athens. To counter the threat from Persia, in 483-482 BC Themistocles proposed strengthening the navy by building 100 triremes, and later led the Athenian fleet at the inconclusive Battle of Artemisium in 480 BC. He went on to triumph at the Battle of Salamis in the same year, where the Persians were decisively defeated, loosing at least 200 ships.

Themistocles helped in rebuilding the city walls of Athens and the fortification of its new harbor at Piraeus between 480 and 477BC. However, his arrogance, and his enthusiasm for taking bribes, led to political isolation and he fled to Persia where he was made welcome. In his absence Themistocles was declared a traitor and his property was confiscated. In Persia he was made governor of Magnesia in Asia Minor.

Although discredited in the end, Themistocles provided great service to Athens and its fleet. He was an astute and innovative politician, and a gifted naval strategist and tactician who eventually succumbed to pride and greed that ultimately led to his downfall.

Top: The funerary stele of Dexilos, killed during a war between Athens and Corinth. This Athenian cemetery at Kerameikos was first established during the governance of Themistocles.

Above: A terracotta pot sherd, dating from the 5th century BC, and bearing the name "Themistocles." This was probably an "ostracon," a form of Greek voting card.

Thutmose III
(1479-1425 BC)
Egyptian Pharaoh

enemy armies. When not on campaign, Thutmose built temples and cities, funded by the plunder gathered from Palestine and Syria.

The reign of Thutmose delivered a period of stability and justice for his people. Neighboring realms were conquered, plundered, and subdued, their cooperation insured by weakening their economies and the taking of hostages. Thutmose himself was a gifted general and a highly competent governor and administrator. He is said to have been the greatest warrior pharaoh, who turned Egypt into a great power.

Left: The Pharaoh Thutmose III wearing a nemes headcloth and the false beard of kingship (a detail from a polished black granite statue in the Temple of Amun at Karnak, Egypt.

Below: A painted relief representation of the Pharaoh Thutmose, dressed for a religious festival.

Thutmose III succeeded his father Thutmose II at a very young age, but ruled only after the death of Queen Hatsheput, his stepmother, who had ruled as regent for twenty years in his place. Early in his reign, Thutmose had to face a rebellion in Syria led by the King of Kadesh. In 1457 BC Thutmose led his 10,000-strong army into Palestine and destroyed the rebel force near Mount Carmel at the Battle of Megiddo.

Campaigning continued for another three decades in Palestine, Syria, and along the Nile into Nubia, where Thutmose is said to have captured 350 cities. However, in later years, military opposition dwindled and these expeditions became more about extracting tribute than defeating

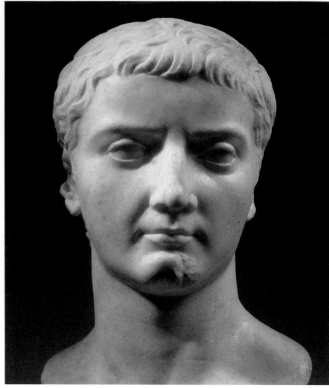

Thutmose I
(also Tutmosis, Tuthmosis)
(c.1525-1512 BC)
Egyptian Pharaoh

Tiberius
(42 BC-37 AD)
Roman Emperor

The third Pharaoh of the 18th dynasty, Thutmose campaigned successfully against Nubia and Syria, and extended the boundaries of Egyptian rule. He was also responsible for many building projects, including the Temple of Karnak. Thutmose was one of the first kings to be buried in the Valley of the Kings.

Above: The Pharaoh Thutmose I, as depicted in a carving and dedication from his sarcophagus. It now forms part of the collection of the Egyptian Museum in Cairo.

Tiberius was one of Rome's greatest generals, whose campaigns along the Danube established Rome's northern frontier. Regarded as a reclusive and reluctant emperor, his rule descended into terror following the death of his son Julius Caesar Drusus in 23 AD. In 26 AD Tiberius exiled himself from Rome but left a strong and united empire after his death.

Above: A Roman marble bust of the youthful Tiberius, produced in the last decade of the 1st century BC, before his accession to the Imperial throne.

Tiglath-Pileser III
(745-727 BC)
King of Assyria

Initially known as Pul or Pulu, after seizing the Assyrian throne in 745 BC Tiglath-Pileser took the name Tiglath-Pileser III. The new king then set about reforming state structure; he reduced the power and provinces of high officials, often appointing eunuchs as governors, thus removing the threat of rival dynasties. Tiglath-Pileser also reorganized the army, doing away with the militia and establishing a powerful standing army of spearmen, horse archers, and chariots, augmented by foreign troops from conquered lands. This army was supported by a new professional bureaucracy and finance system.

Tiglath-Pileser enjoyed a string of military successes. He subdued the Aramaean tribes in Syria, campaigned in the east, overthrowing the tribes in Media, and then defeated Sardur of Urartu, capturing 72,000 prisoners. He defeated Azariah of Judah in 739 BC, captured Damascus and occupied most of Israel in 732 BC, and invaded Babylon between 731 and 729 BC. Tiglath-Pileser died in his palace at Nineveh in 727BC.

Considered one of the most successful generals in military history, Tiglath-Pileser was an energetic and efficient leader and reformer; he founded the Neo-Assyrian Empire and brought it to a peak of efficiency and power. By the time of his death the Assyrian Empire dominated the Near East.

Left: Chariots, horses, and soldiers depicted on one of the bas-relief friezes on the bronze gates at Balawat, Assyria.
Above: Assyrian troops attacking a fortress, in a detail from a limestone relief dating from the 7th century BC, from the Palace of Ashurbanipal in Nineveh.

Tigranes (the Great)
(ruled 95-55 BC)
King of Armenia

Held hostage by the King of Parthia until he was forty, Tigranes extended his empire into Mesopotamia and took the title "king of kings". Eventually Tigranes was defeated by the Romans; he surrendered to Pompey in 66BC and as an ally was allowed to retain remnants his realm.

Right: Tigranes "the Great," King of Armenia, portrayed on an Armenian silver tetradrachma coin of the early 1st century BC.

Tiridates III "the Great"
(reigned 286-330 AD)
King of Armenia

In 287 AD the Roman-educated Tiridates drove the Sassanid Persians from his native Armenia and was proclaimed the state's new ruler. By 301 AD Tiridates had successfully turned Armenia into a pro-Roman Christian state by force of arms, thereby protecting the Eastern Roman Empire from the Parthians and the Persians to the east.

Titus
(39-81 AD, reigned 79-81 AD)
Roman General and Emperor

The eldest son of the Emperor Vespasian, Titus pursued a successful military career before succeeding his father. Most notably he supported his father's bid for power (69 AD), and campaigned in Judea, where he besieged and virtually destroyed Jerusalem (70 AD).

Left: A Roman bust of the Emperor Titus, dating from the late 1st century AD.

Titus Quinctius Flamininus
(228–174 BC)
Republican Roman General and Statesman

Flamininus was a Roman consul by the age of thirty. He defeated Philip V of Macedon at Aous in 196 BC and again at Cynoscephalae the following year. He recovered the conquered Greek cities from Macedonian rule and was hailed as a liberator. In 191 BC Flamininus took part in the Battle of Thermopylae, where Antiochus was defeated.

Trajan
(53-117 AD, reigned 93-117 AD)
Roman Emperor and General

Marcus Ulpius Nerva Traianus was born in the southern Spanish province of Hispania Baetica, the son of a prominent general and Senator. Rather naturally he chose a military career, and in 76 AD he secured an appointment as a military tribune in Syria, the province where his father was governor. He remained in the Eastern Provinces and in Germany, serving with distinction and rising steadily through the ranks. In 89 AD

Left: A Roman marble statue of the Emperor Titus wearing parade armor, late 1st century AD.
Below: A Roman aqueduct dating from reign of Trajan, near Segovia, Spain.

he crushed an army rebellion, and in 91 AD he was nominated as a consul by the Emperor Domitian, and returned to Rome, accompanied by the gifted military engineer Apollodorus of Damascus.

The emperor then sent Trajan to Germany, where he served under the emperor's son and heir, Nerva, a commander who never enjoyed the loyalty of his men. Trajan campaigned against the Germanic Chattii tribe on the eastern bank of the River Rhine, and proved to be a capable army commander. He also employed his friend Apollodorus to help restructure the Limes Romanus, or defensive lines used to guard Rome's Germanic

Above: Trajan's Forum and marketplace in Rome was built under his guidance by the renowned architect Apollodorus of Damascus.
Right: A bronze bust of the Emperor Trajan as he looked in later life (from a Daco-Roman casting from the 3rd century AD, from Ulpia Traiana, Romania).
Following Page: A Roman emperor addressing the citizens of Rome, from a relief of the early 2nd centry AD.

frontier.

The Emperor Domitian, the younger son of Vespasian was generally regarded as a ruthless tyrant, and in 96 AD he was murdered in a palace coup. He was succeeded by Nerva, who proved unable to control the same Praetorian bodyguards who had played a part in the assassination of his father. In order to bolster his popularity with the army Nerva named Trajan as his adoptive son, which elevated Trajan into the Imperial family. When Nerva died in 98 AD the future Emperor Hadrian—then just a legion

Above: Trajan's Column was erected close to the Roman forum in 106-113 AD as a celebration of the emperor's victories over the Dacians. Its surface is decorated with scenes taken from the campaign.

Left: The ruins of the Corinthian-style acropolis known as the Temple of Trajan, built on the instructions of his son Hadrian at Pergamum, Turkey.

commander—raced to Trajan's camp in Germany with the news. Trajan immediately returned to Rome, where he officially succeeded Nerva as emperor. His first act was to dismiss the Praetorian Guard, and to replace them with veterans he could trust.

As an Emperor, Trajan proved to be far more successful than his predecessors. He continued the work begun

by Vespasian in rebuilding the city, most notably adding a new forum, Trajan's Market, and of course Trajan's Column, designed to celebrate his victories in the Dacian Wars. All of these projects were supervised by Apollodorus of Damascus. Trajan also proved to be a skilled administrator, developing good relations with the Senate, and after

Left: The Emperor Trajan in command of his troops during the campaign against the Dacians (in a relief from Trajan's Column).
Below: A further relief from Trajan's Column shows refugees, fleeing from the Dacians, taking refuge behind Roman defenses.

the bloody rule of Domitian he restored peace, order, and security throughout the Empire. Roman historians remembered him as one of the "Five Good Emperors," and even his critics could find little to disapprove of, apart from his penchant for young men and good wine. However, first and foremost Trajan remained a general, and today he is best remembered for his military rather than his civic success.

In 101 AD he led a punitive expedition into Dacia, building a bridge over the River Danube at Viminacium (now in modern Serbia) to allow his legions easy access to the enemy side of the river. Two Roman columns marched into Dacia, and in late 101 AD Trajan managed to bring King Decebalus to battle at Tapae, a Daciuan stronghold. The Dacians remained behind their fortifications, and at first they managed to hold the Roman assault. Then a storm began to rage, which the Dacians took to be a sign of divine displeasure. They retreated, leaving Trajan to claim a decisive victory over his barbarian foes. Trajan then sent his army into winter quarters, but the Dacians were reinforced by the neighboring Sarmatians, and they unexpectedly renewed the offensive. King Decebalus crossed the frozen Danube into Moesia (now Serbia), behind the Roman lines of communication. Trajan gave chase, and caught up with the enemy army at Adamclisi (now Drobuja in Romania). There his legionaries won a costly victory over the barbarians, and drove them back across the river. Trajan then advanced on the Dacian capital of Sarmizegetusa, and Decebalus sued for peace. He was replaced by a puppet king, and Dacia became a Roman province.

Trajan participated in other campaigns during the early 2nd century AD. In 107-108 AD he campaigned in the Middle East, conquering the region of Nabatea (now part of Jordan) and turning it into the Roman province of Arabia Petraea. Then in 113 he conducted his final campaign against the Parthians, a war that culminated in Trajan's capture of the Parthian capital of Susa in 117 AD. It was while he was voyaging home from the Eastern provinces in late 117 AD that he suffered a stroke and died in the port of Selinus, in southern Sicily. He was succeeded by his adoptive son Hadrian, the young officer who had once brought the news of his mentor Nerva's death to him.

Valens
(328-378 AD, reigned 364-378 AD)
Eastern Roman Emperor

In 364 AD the Emperor Valentian I ceded the Eastern portion of his Empire to his brother Valens, a leader of little military experience. Despite this, Valens conducted wars against the Persians and Roman rebels, but at the Battle of Adrianople (378 AD) he suffered a cataclysmic defeat at the hands of the Goths, and died on the battlefield.

Above: The Eastern Roman Emperor Valens, as depicted on a Roman silver aureus coin of the late 4th century AD.

Valentinian I
(Flavius Valentinianus)

(321-375 AD, reigned 364-375 AD)
Western Roman Emperor

Valentinian had a distinguished military career, serving under the Emperors Julian and Jovian. After the death of Jovian, the army declared Valentinian emperor in 364 AD. The empire was divided into his own western empire, which included Italia, Hispania, Gaul, Britain, and Africa, and the eastern empire under his brother Valens, which included the Balkans, Greece, Asia Minor, and Persia.

During Valentinian's reign there was a great deal of

Below: A late 4th century bronze colossus of the Western Roman Emperor Valentian, dominating the center of Barletta in southern Italy.

fighting along the western borders and much time was spent defending and reinforcing these frontiers. In 365 AD Valentinian mustered his army against the Alamanni and in a series of battles he drove them back across the Rhine. In the following year the Alamanni attacked again, sacking the city of Moguntiacum. Valentinian defeated the Alamanni once again, but so great were his losses that further action was not taken, and eventually Valentinian made peace with the Alamanni King Macrianus. In Africa, Valentinian successfully suppressed the revolt of Firmus by dispatching a small force under Theodosius.

Valentinian died in 375 AD, following a violent outburst against emissaries from the Quadi. He was a competent soldier and administrator, and a Christian emperor who permitted considerable religious freedom, but who fell victim to his own fierce temper.

Valerian

(c.200-260 AD, reigned 253-260 AD)
Roman Emperor

A provincial Roman governor, Valerian used his veteran legions to secure the Imperial throne. He then campaigned in Syria, restoring the province to Roman rule, and reconquering Antioch from the Sassanid Persians. However, in 260 AD he was captured by the Persians near Edessa, and he died in captivity soon afterwards.

Gaius Terentius Varro

(c.238-195 BC)
Republican Roman General and Statesman

Varro fought against the Carthaginian general Hannibal at the Battle of Cannae in 216 BC, during the Second Punic War, where the Romans were emphatically defeated. Varro became praetor in 218 BC and later consul. He then traveled to Africa and became ambassador in 200 BC.

Publius Quintilius Varus
(46 BC-9 AD)
Imperial Roman General and Statesman

A Roman politician and general who served under the Emperor Augustus, Varrus is best remembered for losing three Roman legions and his own life at the hands of German tribesmen at the Battle of the Teutoburg Forest (9 AD).

Above: The funerary stele of Marcus Caelius, a Roman legionary who served under Quintilius Varus and who died in battle in the Teutoburg Forest.

Vercingetorix
(d.46 BC)
Chief of the Arverni, Gallic Leader

We know very little about the background of Vercingetorix, save that he was born into a noble family in the Gallic town of Gergovia (now Gergovie), in what is now central France. He belonged to the Arvernii, which had once been the pre-

Above: "The Dying Gaul," a Gallo-Roman bronze statuette found in the forum of Alesia—the site of Julius Caesar's great victory over Vercingetorix.

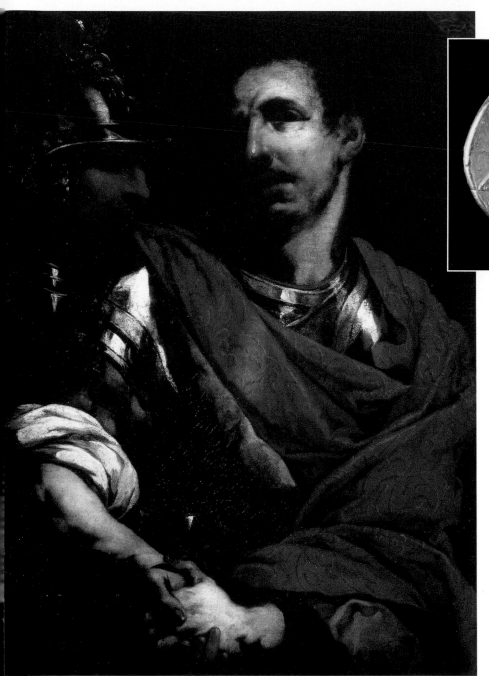

Above: Vercingetorix, Chief of the Averni, as depicted on a Gallic gold *stater* coin of the mid-1st century BC.
Left: Vercingetorix after his capture by the Romans, from a 17th century painting by a Venetian artist.

eminent tribe in Gaul, but whose standing had fallen by the mid-1st century BC. When Julius Caesar launched his invasion of Gaul in 58 BC the Arvernii initially welcomed the Romans, who had defended the Gallic tribes from a major incursion by the Germans. However, it soon became clear that Caesar was bent on conquest. By the winter of 54-53 BC those Gallic tribes who had survived the onslaught had risen against the invaders. Naturally Caesar referred to this resistance as a "revolt." Although the Romans managed to crush Gallic resistance by the end of 53 BC, Vercingetorix continued to inspire the Arvernii to take up arms during the winter of 53-52 BC, and encouraged other tribes to follow his lead.

Caesar was in Cisalpine Gaul when news of the rising reached him in early 52 BC. He immediately marched on the Arvernii capital of Gerovia. Vercingetorix was well aware that the Gauls were unable to face the Romans in open battle, so he adopted Fabian tactics, harassing the Romans and denying them supplies while avoiding a pitched battle. Consequently, while Caesar captured the city of Avaricum (now Bourges) without much difficulty, Vercingetorix managed to surprise the Romans outside Gerovia, forcing Caesar to give up the siege. The two sides then began a protracted campaign of marches and counter-marches, but in late 52 BC Caesar finally cornered Vercingetorix in the hilltop stronghold of Alesia. The Romans laid siege to the fortress, and managed to defeat an army sent to its relief. Faced with starvation, Vercingetorix had no option but to surrender.

The capture of Vercingetorix led to the collapse of organized resistance, and Caesar soon managed to subjugate Gaul completely. During this time Vercingetorix was held prisoner in Rome until 46 BC, when Caesar held his Gallic "triumph." Vercingetorix was duly marched through the streets as Caesar's captive, and then executed.

Right: The imposing statue of Vercingetorix, Chief of the Averni, erected in 1865 on Le Mons Auxois, at Alesia (now Alise Sainte Reine), France.

Lucius Verus
(130-169 AD, reigned 161-169 AD)
Roman Emperor

Vespasian
(17-79AD, reigned 70-79 AD)
Imperial Roman General and Emperor

Groomed from birth to be emperor, Verus shared the throne with his adoptive brother Marcus Aurelius. During his reign he led campaigns against the Parthians (162-164 AD) and the Germans (168-169 AD), proving to be an excellent military commander.

Above: A Roman marble bust of the Emperor Verus, late 2nd century AD.

Titus Flavius Vespasianus, the man who seized the Roman Imperial throne, was born in Southern Italy, the son of a minor official. However, his uncle was a senator, who helped secure the young Vespasian a commission as a

Above: A Roman marble bust of the Emperor Vespasian, late 1st century AD, recovered from the forum of Hippone (now Annaba), Algeria).

Above: The Emperor Vespasian, as depicted on a Roman bronze *sestertius* coin of the late 1st century AD.
Left: Roman marble bust of the Emperor Vespasian, late 1st century AD.

military tribune. Vespasian served in Thrace and Africa, then began climbing the political ladder, becoming a praetor in 40 AD. The following year Vespasian was appointed as the legate in command of the II Legion ("Augusta"), stationed on the German frontier. Emperor Claudius earmarked the legion to spearhead the Roman invasion of Britain, and so in the summer of 43 AD the force landed in Kent, alongside the men of three other legions. Vespasian distinguished himself during the battles against the British tribes defending the Rivers Medway and Thames.

Vespasian's commander, Aulus Paulus, continued on to the north, leaving Vespasian and his II Legion to march west—the young Vespasian's his first independent command. He performed brilliantly, winning a string of battles, capturing twenty hill-forts including Hod Hill and Maiden Castle, and subduing all the British tribes he encountered. After securing the southwest of Britain he established a new legionary base at Isca Dumnoniorum (now Exeter). This campaign earned him the right to hold a triumph on his return to Rome. His triumph helped insure his election as consul in 51 AD, albeit that the rank was by now largely titular. He then retired from public life for over a decade until 63 AD, when he was appointed governor of Africa province (now Tunisia). Instead of making a profit from his governorship he actually lost money, forcing him to set up a business supplying transport mules. Naturally this earned him the

nickname mule-driver with his men.

He then provided an escort for the Emperor Nero as the Imperial court traveled through Greece, but Vespasian fell from favor, and consequently lost much of his political influence. However, he was saved from obscurity by the Jewish Revolt, during which outbreak Vespasian was sent to Judea to restore order. He crushed the rebellion with vigorous brutality, pinning down the rebels in the stronghold of Masada, and then crushing them. Thousands of Jews were killed throughout the province; their towns were destroyed and the survivors were exiled. Having pacified the province he ruled over it as procurator, and despite his brutal military methods he proved an able and fair administrator. He also controlled some of the most experi-

enced Roman legionaries in the empire.

His chance to use them came in 68 AD, following the forced suicide of the Emperor Nero. A civil war erupted, while there was a struggle for power known as the "Year of the Four Emperors," during which the four most powerful commanders in the empire vied for control. First Servius Sulpicius Galba was declared the new emperor and seized control of Rome. One of his first acts was to place his supporter Aulus Vitellius in command of the legions in Germany, who were on the verge of rebellion. Vitellius promptly turned on Galba, and led the rebel legions on Rome. Shortly afterwards Galba was killed on the streets of Rome during a coup orchestrated by Marcus Salvius Otho. The latter was declared the new

emperor, and he marched north to confront Vitellius. He was duly defeated at the Battle of Bedriacum, and committed suicide shortly afterwards. Vitellius was duly declared the new emperor.

Vespasian then made his move in 70 AD, and was proclaimed a rival emperor. He also controlled Rome's grain shipments from Egypt, and without food the people rioted. The German legions then declared themselves loyal to Vespasian and

Above: Construction began on the Colosseum in Rome during the reign of Vespasian, although the work was finally completed in 80 AD, a year after his death.
Following page: The Emperor Vespasian supervising the construction of the Colosseum in Rome, in a painting by 17th century artist Charles de Lafosse.

marched south again, defeating Vitellius in battle. Meanwhile, Vespasian landed in Italy and captured Rome. Vitellius tried to hide, but was hunted down and killed. This left Vespasian as the unchallenged Roman emperor.

As emperor, Vespasian proved to be a sound ruler, and the Roman Empire prospered during his nine years on the throne. He strengthened Rome's frontiers, ordered the launch of Agricola's expedition into northern Britain, and reformed the finances of the empire that had suffered considerable neglect under Nero. By offering patronage to scholars he also ensured his largely favorable historical legacy. Vespasian was also responsible for the urban regeneration of much of Roma, a project that included the building of the Coliseum. He

Above: The triumph of the Emperors Titus and Vespasian, in a painting by Giulio Romano, c.1537.

managed to foil at least one plot against him, but by the time of his death in 79 AD his hold over the empire was secure. This security was demonstrated when Vespasian was succeeded without contest by his son Titus Flavius.

Viriathus
(c.139 BC)
Chief of the Lusatians and Spanish Leader

A tribal leader who attempted to defend his homeland against the Romans, Viriathus used guerrilla tactics to wear down his enemies. He proved a highly successful commander, but Lusatian resistance collapsed following his assassination by Roman agents.

Left: The death of Viriathus, in a late 19th century painting by Frederico de Madrazo.

Vortigern (also Vortiger or Vortigen)
(c.450 AD)
Romano-British Warlord

Vortigern is a semi-legendary figure, a warlord who may have lived in Britain in the fifth century. He is said to have invited Saxon mercenaries into Britain to fight the Picts, only for them to rebel against him and establish their own kingdom in eastern England. Gildas describes Vortigern as a usurper, possibly against Roman rule; however, Bede depicts him as king of the British people. Other later

Left: The Briton Vortigern, semi-legendary warlord, was mentioned in this 13th century illustrated manuscript listing the genealogy of the Kings of England.

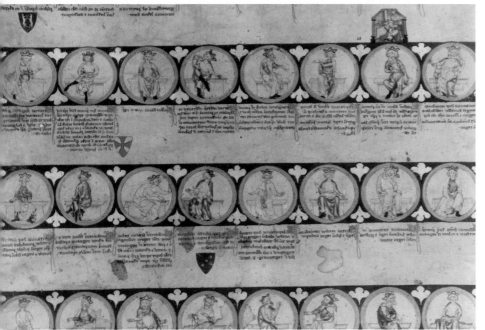

accounts even accuse Vortigern of incest and being a traitor and an oath-breaker. The Anglo-Saxon Chronicles add more detail to his account, describing how Vortigern led the British people against the armies of Hengest and Horsa.

Geoffrey of Monmouth's account was written centuries later and drew on existing oral traditions as well as previous written accounts. Monmouth manages to provide more detail than the previous stories and claims that Vortigern was the successor to Constans, the son of the emperor Constantine III. Also in Monmouth's account, Vortigern marries Rowen, daughter of Hengest. It is not clear whether Vortigern was simply a legendary figure or a real person who attracted many stories to his name. Whatever the truth, stories of Vortigern achieved great popularity in England, Wale,s and the rest of Europe.

Wallia (or Valia)
(reigned 415-419 AD)
King of the Visigoths

Wallia became ruler of the Visigoths following the assassination of their previous king in 415 AD. Wallia's first act was to make peace with the Romans, and he established a permanent court in Tolouse. In 418 AD he campaigned against the Vandals in Spain and consequently he greatly increased the size of his kingdom.

王昭
位，是ン
廷的大木
帝的母亲、
他人都封
大将军。

Wang Mang (also Jujun)
(45 BC-23 AD, ruled 9-23 AD)
Chinese Xin Ruler

Having seized the Imperial Han throne in a coup, Wang Mang provoked the nomadic Xiongnu people of Central Asia, and their frequent raids, coupled with a string of natural disasters, ignited a widespread rebellion. China's only Xin emperor died defending his palace from the mob, and on his death the Han dynasty was restored to power.

Above: Wang Mang, emperor of the Xin Dynasty, from a Chinese manuscript.

Xenophon

(431–355 BC)
Athenian General and Author

Xenophon was born in Athens into a wealthy aristocratic family. He is thought to have begun his *Hellenica (A History of My Times)* between 404 and 401 BC. He joined the army of Cyrus the Younger and fought in the battle of Cunaxa in 401 BC, in which Cyrus was killed and his army was broken. Without leadership and in hostile territory, Xenophon was elected general and led the Greek mercenaries, known as the "Ten Thousand," in a perilous march north to the Black Sea, repelling numerous attacks from local tribesmen before reaching the Greek colony of Trapezus.

Xenophon recorded the journey in his *Anabasis (The Expedition)*, which was used as a guide by Alexander the Great during his march into Persia. He went on to serve in Thrace under King Seuthes, but then transferred to Spartan service under King Agesilaus. Xenophon left Sparta in the aftermath of the Spartan defeat at Leuctra in 371 BC, and then lived in Corinth for some years. Xenophon returned to Athens in 365 BC where he finished the *Hellenica* shortly before his death in 355 BC. Undoubtedly a skilful cavalryman and resourceful leader, Xenophon was however a less reliable historian who allowed his own political bias to cloud his work.

Above: The Greek philosopher Socrates, in conversation with the theologian Euthyphro and the mercenary general Xenophon, depicted in a 19th century neo-classical drawing.

Xerxes "the Great"
(reigned 486-465 BC)
King of Persia

Xerxes was the son of King Darius "the Great" and Atossam, the daughter of King Cyrus. When Darius died he was planning an expedition into Greece, but on his accession Xerxes faced more immediate problems. The

Right: Xerxes "the Great," King of Persia, followed by two servants, in a 5th century BC relief from Persepolis, Iran.
Below: Xerxes "the Great," depicted killing a lion during a hunt (in a relief on a gate leading into the Hall of a Hundred Columns, Persepolis).

death of Darius prompted revolts in the key Persian provinces of Babylon and Egypt, both of which were crushed within two years by Darius and his Persian army, although resentment continued to simmer in Babylonia until at least 479 BC. As a result of this insurrection he stopped referring to himself as "King of Babylon," preferring the title of "King of Persia," or even "King of Countries" (i.e., the known world).

In 483 BC Xerxes began preparing for war with the Greek States, a punitive campaign designed to punish the Greeks for their successful opposition to his father. This resulted in the Greek victory at Marathon (490 BC). Military contingents were gathered from throughout the Persian Empire, and bridges were constructed over the Hellespont (now known as the Dardanelles). Meanwhile, his diplomats secured the support of several Greek cities, including Thebes and Argos. When the campaign was launched in the spring of 480 BC it was estimated that Xerxes had as many as two million men under his command.

This great Persian host was halted at the Pass of Thermopylae by a small Greek force commanded by King Leonidas of Sparta. Repeated attempts to dislodge the Greek defenders were repulsed, and victory was achieved only when the Persians learned of a mountain path that allowed them to bypass the Greek position. Leonidas was killed, alongside the "300 Spartans" who formed the core of his force. Xerxes pressed south to Athens, which he captured, driving the

Greeks south to the Isthmus of Corinth. At that point the Persian king brought his fleet into action, sending it south to engage the smaller Athenian fleet off Salamis. Against all predictions the Persian armada was decisively defeated by the Athenians, as Xerxes watched the sea battle from the shore. In disgust, the king returned to Babylon with most of his army, and the Persian force that remained in Greece was defeated in

early 479 BC at the Battle of Plataea. Little is known of Xerxes' final years, other than that in 465 BC he was murdered in a coup led by his chief advisor, Artabanus.

Above: The remains of the once magnificent Hall of a Hundred Columns amid the ruins of Xerxes' 5th century BC palace.
Following page: Xerxes, King of Persia, on the banks of the Hellespont, in an early 19th century painting by Jean Adrien Guignet

項羽

万大军于

項羽得矢

函谷

Xiang Yu
(232-202 BC)
Chinese General

A superb general and heroic leader who carved out an empire in only a few years, Xiang was considered impetuous and less skilled in diplomacy and administrative affairs, and thus failed to maintain his realm. He eventually succumbed to rebellion and was defeated by the Han. According to legend he killed himself by decapitation.

Left: Xiang Yu, from a Chinese manuscript. He was out-fought by his Han rivals during the Wars of the three Kingdoms.

Zenobia
(reigned 267-274 AD)
Queen of Palmyra

The "Warrior Queen" of King Odaenathus succeeded her husband as ruler of the Palymyran Kingdom in 267 AD. In 269 AD her armies conquered Egypt, but five years later she was defeated by the Emperor Aurelian. Zenobia was taken to Rome, and died in exile.

Zhang Liang
(d. 189 AD)
Chinese Han Strategist

Although he was never seen as a general, Zhang Liang was a grand strategist, who served Liu Bang, the Emperor Gaozu of Han. His sound advice—said to have had mystical roots—played a major part in the successful establishment of the Han Dynasty.

Above: Ziang Lang is widely regarded as a Chinese strategic thinker second only to Sun Tzu.

Zhao Yun
(d. 229 AD)
Chinese Shu Han General

A leading military figure in Chinese history, Zhao Yun served the warlord Liu Bei, founder of the Shu Han dynasty. He won a surprise victory over Liu Bei's enemy, Cao Cao, at the Battle of Hanshui (219 AD), achieved through a combination of courage, cunning, and audacity.

Left: Zhao Yun receiving the surrender of one of Cao Cao's generals, in this 16th century Chinese print.

Zhou Yu
(175-210 AD)
Chinese Wu General and Strategist

One of the most celebrated military strategists in Chinese history, Zhou Yu fought for the Eastern Wu Emperor Sun Quan, his most notable success being the orchestration of the victory over the warlord Cao Cao at the Battle of Red Cliffs.

Left: Zhou Yu, refusing to receive an envoy from a rival Chinese warlord, a scene depicted in a modern Chinese postage stamp.

50 分 中国邮政 CHINA

1992 – 9   蒋干盗书   (4-3) T

Index